THE CREATIVE CHRISTIAN WOMAN

DISCOVER AND UNLOCK THE GOD-GIVEN CREATIVITY HIDDEN WITHIN YOU!

JENNIFER CARTER

Copyright © 2025 by Jennifer Carter

All rights reserved.

No part of this book may be reproduced in any form or by any electronic or mechanical means, including information storage and retrieval systems, without written permission from the author, except for the use of brief quotations in a book review.

Any stories or examples depicted in this book are fictional unless otherwise indicated. Any similarity to actual persons, living or dead, is purely coincidental.

All Scripture quotations, unless otherwise indicated, are taken from the World English Bible (WEB).

Scripture quotations marked (TPT) are from The Passion Translation®. Copyright © 2017, 2018 by Passion & Fire Ministries, Inc. Used by permission. All rights reserved. ThePassionTranslation.com

Please note, this book is written in British English , so you may notice some variations in spelling compared to American English. I hope you'll embrace these subtle differences in spelling as you read.

This devotional shares my personal reflections and understanding of Scripture. As with any Bible study material, I encourage readers to examine the Scriptures for themselves and seek God's wisdom directly.

By reading this book, you acknowledge that you are responsible for your own decisions, actions, and results. You agree not to hold the author or publisher liable for any outcomes resulting from applying the information in this book.

CONTENTS

Introduction	v
1. Who Killed Your Creativity?	1
2. What's Shaped You?	3
3. My Own Creative Journey	7
4. What Exactly is Creativity Anyway?	14
5. God's Creative Blueprint	22
6. What is the Purpose of Creativity?	29
7. What's Your Dream?	39
8. Hearing God's Whisper	50
9. Fear: The Enemy of Creativity	64
10. Breaking Through Creative Barriers	76
11. Build Your Creative Confidence	86
12. Removing the Boulders	94
13. Living A Life of Creativity	102
14. Your Journey Begins	111
Becoming a Christ Follower	113
About The Author	117
One More Thing	119

INTRODUCTION

When I think back to my school days, there's one memory that stands out vividly. Receiving a 12% in a creative arts class was a defining moment for me.

Twelve percent! At the time, I took it as evidence that I simply wasn't a "*creative person*". Creativity was for other people, the artsy types, not for me.

But once I became a Christian, I began to question what I'd believed about myself. What if being creative was about more than natural talent or skills?

Those questions sent me on a journey of rediscovering my creativity that has touched every area of my life.

From writing books, to making YouTube videos, to finding fresh ways to express my creativity, I've discovered the joy of embracing my God-given identity.

No longer believing the lie that I'm not creative, I now see myself as a much-loved daughter of my creative Father, called to join Him in bringing more beauty and truth into the world.

I've discovered that creativity is a powerful way to connect with and reflect the heart of our creative Heavenly Father.

In this book, I want to bust the myth that some of us "*just aren't creative*".

By digging into what the Bible reveals about God's creative nature and our own identity as His image-bearers, we'll see that creativity isn't just a bonus, but a vital part of our walk with Jesus.

He has given each of us unique passions, perspectives and points of view. I truly believe God wants to spark and unleash creativity in you - not just for your own enjoyment and fulfilment, but ultimately for His glory.

It's time to embrace the fullness of who you were made to be, as a creative daughter made in the image of our infinitely creative God.

Are ready to break free from the lie that you've been told?

Then let's dive in together!

ONE
WHO KILLED YOUR CREATIVITY?

Elizabeth Gilbert, bestselling author of Eat, Pray, Love, once did a survey on creativity. The survey results showed that 85% of men and women remembered a shaming event from school which affected them all their life. For 50% of these, those shame wounds were around creativity.

If you don't feel artistic or creative, it's likely that's because the education system taught you to believe that.

The education system has a very narrow view of creativity. If you don't fit the mould, or excel at so-called 'creative' subjects, you can come away believing that you're not creative.

Nothing could be further from the truth. The Bible tells us of a God who is creative at the very core of his being.

At the very beginning of God's story, we're told of a God who delighted in His creation. He exults over each creative act.

He revels in the giving of light, the making of the sea and the land, the creation of the sun, moon and stars. After each, He expresses that 'it is good'.

This tells us of a Father who takes delight in creating. As His children, we're made in his likeness (Genesis 1:27). That means that creativity is embedded in our DNA. It's hidden deep within us, whether we're aware of it or not.

Creativity is part of our DNA as children of God, yet so many of us have lost touch with this vital part of ourselves or been told to ignore it.

To understand why, we need to look back at the experiences that have shaped us and the messages we've accepted about our creative potential.

Over To You

What messages about creativity did you receive growing up?

....

....

....

Can you recall a specific moment when you decided you *"weren't creative"*?

....

....

....

TWO
WHAT'S SHAPED YOU?

On a scale of 1 to 10, how would you rate your creativity right now? Perhaps you feel as if you haven't got a creative bone in your body.

Maybe you've even said as much to those around you? Perhaps you enjoyed being creative as a child, but someone made you feel ashamed of your efforts or made you doubt your creative abilities.

Maybe the school system squashed rather than encouraged your creativity.

Turning Points in Your Creative Journey

Can you identify a moment when you gave up on the idea of being creative? Was there a specific instance when someone's words or actions caused you to feel ashamed or embarrassed and walk away from your creative self?

Perhaps you knew someone really creative and felt you couldn't compare. Maybe you heard words that made you doubt your own creativity.

You might have believed creativity wasn't part of your family's path to success, or set such high standards for yourself that you ruled out even trying.

Or maybe you know someone who's so creative that you feel you can't match their high standard? Perhaps you've dreamt of being more creative but don't know where to start. Maybe you enjoy expressing your creativity but are fearful of taking it further.

Breaking Free from Creative Limitations

It's time to restore what you lost along the way. It's time to discover a confidence in your creative abilities and identify the beliefs that have been holding you back.

Whatever your experience, you'll discover that creativity is not just a gift for the chosen few, but a God-given birthright for every one of His children - including you.

We'll explore what the Bible has to say about you and about creativity. You'll uncover the truth about who God says you are and the amazing creative potential He's placed within you.

You'll discover the creativity that's been lying dormant inside you and learn what's been holding you back. We'll tackle the lies and misconceptions that have kept you from fully embracing your creative identity.

You'll understand how you can push past your fears and remove obstacles that stand in your way. You'll gain the tools and confidence you need to start walking in the creative freedom God intends for you.

You'll learn how to take the next steps to embrace the God-given creative gift inside you. Get ready to say yes to the creative dreams and desires God has placed in your heart!

And you'll experience the joy that comes from simple acts of creativity. As you begin to express your God-given creativity, you'll find a fresh sense of purpose, fulfilment and connection with your Creator.

If you're ready to take the first step on the journey to understanding and embracing your God-given creativity, let's start by seeing how our early experiences and words spoken over us have shaped our beliefs and kept us back from fulfilling our creative potential.

It's time to break free from the creative limitations that others have placed on you and to start seeing yourself as God does.

Over To You

What score did you give yourself, and why?

....

....

....

Can you identify a moment when you gave up on the idea of being creative?

....

....

....

THREE
MY OWN CREATIVE JOURNEY

This is my story. It's about my journey from maths geek to creative entrepreneur.

If I can do it, I believe that anyone can. Yes, I know everyone says that, but believe me, it's true.

As a teenager, if you'd asked me if I was creative, I wouldn't have hesitated for a moment to respond. My answer would have been an emphatic no.

I did well at school and college. I loved like maths and statistics, but when it came to arts and crafts lessons, I couldn't wait for the lesson to end. I hated every second.

My report card, at age 12, showed the abysmal score of 12% in needlework. My grade in art wasn't much better. The best thing my teachers could say about me was that I was 'enthusiastic'.

My score of 12% in my needlework test

The teachers made me feel ashamed that, despite my efforts, I was failing in their subjects. Worse still was the fact that I was powerless to do anything about it. No amount of effort could change the fact that I didn't seem to have an arty gene in my body.

I did what any smart kid would do my and focused on the subjects I was good at. My school reports show that instead of trying harder in creative subjects, I played around in class.

I must have worked hard enough in some subjects because I got the grades needed for a place at university. It was a very proud moment for both myself, my parents and my sister when I graduated with a degree in Statistics.

Looking back now, it was easy to see that my sister was the arty one. I used to think that she lucked out in the genetic gene pool and got all the arty genes going.

Unlike me, she aced all the arty subjects going on to do a degree in graphic design and become an art teacher. When I compared myself to my creative sister, I was a complete dunce. Her creativity came effortlessly. I will confess that I had a severe case of 'comparisonitis'.

I had convinced myself that my left brain's dominance in the areas of maths and logic was fixed, and that my right brain's lack of creativity and artistic ability was immoveable. I didn't yet realise that my brain could change, grow and develop.

So I pigeonholed myself, put myself in a box that I was comfortable with. I was the one was good at maths, logic, statistics even but I knew that art and creative subjects just weren't for me.

Even though I didn't pursue creative activities, I enjoyed experiencing creativity of others. Deep down, I longed to be more creative, but felt powerless to change the cards life had dealt me. It felt as if I didn't have a creative bone in my body.

Years passed, and I settled into the belief that I simply wasn't a creative person. In that time, I'd become a Christian, got married and had children. But then, one day, everything changed.

The breakthrough happened at church one Sunday morning. Our preacher was a real theologian who knew his Bible inside and out. He spoke about how we're all made to be creative.

To be honest, I was only half listening to his message. My mind was wandering, thinking more about what was going to be for Sunday lunch.

Did you ever listen to the preacher and found· yourself thinking if doesn't apply to you? It's like a child who puts their fingers in their ears so that they can't hear what you're saying. That's exactly what I was doing that morning. I found myself thinking of these people who I thought needed to hear this message.

I didn't imagine that his message could apply to me. I'd spent years knowing that I wasn't creative and, to be honest, got comfortable with the idea. So what the preacher said next made me stop and think. "*If you ever booked a holiday and it's not been a package holiday and you put it all together, then you're creative*".

Boom! That made me sit up and think. Thoughts of my Sunday lunch went out the window. I realised that, yes, I had done that, not once, but many times. This was totally unexpected, my lightbulb moment. Once I heard what he said, I couldn't unhear it.

In a moment, my eyes were opened to the truth. The preachers words kept going around in my mind. I was creative! Me! I could scarcely believe it. This changed everything.

I didn't fit into the teacher's neat pigeonholes, but that didn't mean I wasn't creative. I couldn't paint, sew or bake, but that didn't mean I wasn't creative. My best drawing looked like a five-year old's stick man drawing, but that didn't mean I wasn't creative.

For so long, I'd lived with the shame of not being a creative person in a society which rejoices in creativity. But now I realised that all these years, that I'd believed a lie.

At that moment I realised that there was so much more to creativity than I'd ever imagined. And I finally understood the truth about myself. I realised that there's a God-given creativity inside everyone. That creativity is bursting to get out. That there's a joy that we'll only ever know, when we embrace and express that creativity. And that creativity brings joy not only to us, but to God's heart.

All that stuff that I'd read about left and right brains was true. But I'd allowed myself to be limited by it.

My Story Continues

Since that revelation my life has changed completely. I've learnt to embrace and express my creativity in so many different ways. It's hard to know where to start, because creativity now infuses every area of my life.

I own and run a creative business. I've written poems, songs and books, made videos, created t-shirt designs and learnt to love baking. I've learnt to narrate audiobooks, knitted scarves, made beeswax candles and written a cookbook.

Much to my surprise, I have a successful YouTube channel, with 16,000 subscribers, at the time of writing, which I'm proud to have created.

But my story's not over yet - my journey into creativity continues each and every day. Creativity brings me great joy. It's also great way to express yourself during difficult times. There's nothing like making a traybake or chocolate torte to help you forget your problems and focus on the simple pleasures of the moment.

So if you, like me, have believed the lie that you're not creative - I want to invite you on a journey of rediscovery. It's time to reclaim the creative birthright that God has placed inside you.

As we learn to embrace and express our unique creativity, we'll experience a deeper joy and connection with our Creator.

The best part? The journey is just beginning.

Over To You

Think of and list three people you know who you think are creative:

....

....

....

What is it about these individuals that makes them seem creative to you?

....

....

....

How does their creativity make you feel? How do they inspire you to embrace your own creativity?

....

....

....

FOUR
WHAT EXACTLY IS CREATIVITY ANYWAY?

The voices of our past may have convinced us that we're not creative, but the Bible tells a different story.

From the very first page, we see a God who delights in the creative process and infuses His creation with purpose and meaning.

Creativity was present at the very beginning. We see it in the first moments of creation. In Genesis 1:1, we read: "*In the beginning, God created the heavens and the earth.*"

These are the very first words in our Bibles. They tell us of a God who creates. Not only that, but we learn that He loves what He creates. In Genesis 1:10, we read that "*God saw that it was good.*"

Our Heavenly Father didn't need an audience. The simple act of creating, in itself, brought joy and satisfaction. This tells us something profound about the nature of creativity - it is inherently good and fulfilling, regardless of external validation or recognition.

So what exactly is creativity, and what does it mean to be creative?

The English language falls short when it comes to defining creativity. The Oxford Dictionary defines creativity as "*the use of imagination or original ideas to create something; inventiveness.*"

Lawrence Osborn, author of Creative Christianity, puts it this way: "*Creativity is my ability to bring things that are both new and good into my world.*"

By the way, isn't saying "*Creative Christianity*" a bit like saying "*Loving Christianity*"? Or like saying "*short dwarf*" or "*big giant*"? Creativity is wrapped up in our identity as Christians. To think of ourselves without it is unimaginable.

To put it another way, creativity is creating something from nothing, or taking something in one form and transforming it.

It's the act of bringing into existence that which did not exist before, or giving new meaning and purpose to that which already exists.

Who or what do you think of when you think about a creative person?

Many of us, myself included, have a long-held and narrow view of creativity. We have clearly defined boundaries of what it is and isn't.

We may limit creativity to those whose creativity is obvious. We think of those who create amazing art, have a gift with crafts, or have a flair for decorating their home. Or of great musicians, artists, movie directors, writers, or playwrights.

Yet creativity is so much more than this. Once we look around, we can see that creativity is everywhere. It's woven into the fabric of our daily lives, often in ways we overlook or take for granted.

In the parable of the talents, each man was given some talents. Some had more, some had less, but each was called to account for being faithful with what they had been given.

Brenda Ueland grasped this truth about our potential when she said, "*Everybody is talented because everybody who is human has something to express.*"

Let's go back to Osborn's definition of "*creating something from nothing.*" That could be taking an idea and bringing it to life. It could be taking some raw materials and forming them into something new.

Creativity is the act of taking something in one form and making it into another form.

Doesn't that mean that baking a cake, making jam, knitting a garment, or writing a poem are creative acts? So would organising a day out or planning an event.

How about starting up a new venture or playing games with your kids or grandkids? What about coming up with a different way of solving a problem?

This playful spirit of creativity was expressed well by Mary Lou Cook, *"Creativity is inventing, experimenting, growing, taking risks, breaking rules, making mistakes and having fun."*

All these bring things which are both new and good into the world, or create something that did not exist before. They are all expressions of the creative spirit God has placed within us.

Using this broader definition, creating a meal from a list of ingredients is a creative act. Taking a photo or filming a video is a creative act. Planning a party or vacation is a creative act.

Albert Einstein captured this wider view of creativity, when he said, *"creativity is seeing what everyone else has seen, and thinking what no one else has thought."* His words help us see that creativity is about so much more than making art.

Are you starting to see how creativity might encompass more than you first imagined?

These may not be what we have traditionally thought of as creative acts, yet, just as Osborn said, each one of them brings something new and good into the world. We need a better understanding of the breadth and depth of creativity.

On the opposite page are some words that help capture the spirit of creativity. Maybe one or more of these words will inspire you or stir your heart.

As you read these words, allow the Holy Spirit to speak to you. Make special note of any that resonate especially or stir long-buried feelings.

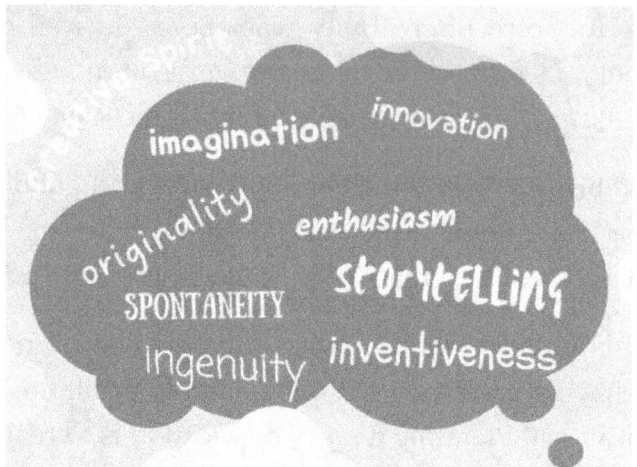

Which of these words resonated with you or stirred your heart? Make a note of them - I believe that God is already speaking to you, showing what He's laid on your heart.

What might creativity look like for you, personally?

We encounter creativity every day. It's all around us, and within us. Creativity is an act that has a purpose, even when we're just doing it for our own enjoyment and appreciation. It's creating something that did not exist before, bringing something new and good into the world.

Maybe you're reading this and feel as if you don't have a creative bone in your body. If that's you, take a moment to think back to your childhood. Almost everything you did as a child was a creative act.

Did you make dens and mud pies or play with Lego? Did you paint pictures, squish and shape play dough, or make daisy chains? Did you create imaginary worlds for your toys or pretend you were something or someone else? Maybe you escaped to the worlds of books, living others' adventures in your imagination?

If you're thinking that creativity really isn't for you, no problem. I get where you're coming from. Perhaps, like children sometimes do, your fingers are in your ears, not wanting to hear any of this. But let me tell you about Michelle.

I had the privilege of working with Michelle when she was working as P.A. to our church leader. She had a gift for organising both the church calendar and its leader.

Yet Michelle never felt creative in herself. That is, until one day when she felt God speak to her, giving her a *"heavenly blueprint"* for a Christian women's event.

Michelle was visibly excited, especially because she'd never "felt" creative. Here was an obviously creative event for which God had given her the blueprint, an event which He'd called her to organise and make happen.

She approached the event with some trepidation. Would it all go well? Had she really heard from God?

On the day, the event went without a hitch. The women who'd attended came away talking about how they'd met with God in a powerful way. Michelle's faithfulness blessed not only herself but many women in the church.

This was the first step on Michelle's creative journey. It was a revelation to her that God could use her for something so imaginative and creative.

Creativity had lain dormant inside her all these years. When God spoke, Michelle followed through, in spite of her fears. Maybe you're feeling like Michelle did before the moment when God spoke to her.

Since you're reading this book, it's my guess that God's already been speaking to you. If it was a gift, perhaps someone who can see your inner creativity is trying to encourage you out of your shell? Like your Heavenly Father, you are creative at the very core of your being. You're made in His image!

It won't be easy or comfortable realising that you've believed the lies about who you are for all these years. It's not easy starting out as a *"beginner"* at anything, even less so as adults. You're out of your comfort zone, can feel out of control, and are wholly reliant on God.

Hang on a minute, isn't *"wholly reliant on God"* where you should aim to be every hour of every day? Yes, I know it's not always quite that easy, but you get my drift. If you could do it yourself, you wouldn't need God.

It's when we have to rely on Him that we grow closer, learning so much in the process, not to mention seeing the way He so often comes through for us in amazing ways.

Do you still feel reticent about the idea of your identity as an inherently creative being? If that's you, why not start by exploring the creativity of others?

Music, art, books, movies, and plays are all ways to experience and be part of the act of creativity. You can experience creativity almost without having to lift a finger!

Creativity begets creativity. It stirs something deep within us. Immerse yourself more and more in the creativity of others. As you do so, you may begin to feel stirred to express yourself through creative acts. Why not take small steps of faith and see what God will do?

God is longing to do something in and through you. He's just waiting for you to take that first step.

Over To You

Did you identify with any part of Michelle's story?

....
....
....

What creative thing have you always wanted to try but were afraid to start?

....
....
....

How might your life look if you truly believed that God wanted to you to embrace your creative potential?

....
....
....

FIVE
GOD'S CREATIVE BLUEPRINT

To fully embrace our creativity, we need to know who we are in God's eyes and why He has given us creative gifts. So, let's look at what the Bible says about creativity and how it relates to us as individuals.

By exploring these examples, we can gain a greater understanding of our own creative potential and the role that creativity plays in our relationship with God.

In the very first pages of our Bibles, we see God the Creator, bringing forth the universe and all that is in it. We see Him fashioning each one of us in His image. This means that creativity is not just a talent or a skill, but an essential part of who we are as God's children.

Throughout the Old Testament, we witness God's creativity in the design of the tabernacle, the beauty of the psalms and proverbs, and the vivid imagery used by the prophets to convey His messages.

In the life and ministry of Jesus Christ we see creativity in His parables, miracles, and teachings. He transforms ordinary things like bread, fish, and water into powerful symbols of spiritual truth.

Jesus' life, death, and resurrection were the ultimate creative masterpiece, showing us the depths of God's love and His power to make all things new.

As we explore these biblical truths, my prayer is that you'll begin to see yourself in a new light - as a beloved child of God, chosen and appointed to carry on His creative work in the world.

Get ready to claim your creative inheritance and step into all that God has called you to be!

Designed To Create

The story of creation tells us not just about the creation of the world, but about our identity.

The Bible tells us that we're made in the image and likeness of our heavenly Father. "*God created man in his own image. In God's image he created him*" (Genesis 1:27).

There is so much more to this creation story. In these words we discover a profound revelation of who we are. Just like our Father, we were born to create.

To understand our creative inheritance, we must first look at

God Himself - a Creator who creates with purpose, imagination, and joy.

From the very first chapter of Genesis, we see a God who delights in the creative process and infuses His creation with purpose and meaning.

In the very beginning of the Bible, we're told of a God who creates something from nothing. He brought order out of disorder. "*Now the earth was formless and empty, darkness was over the surface of the deep, and the Spirit of God was hovering over the waters*" (Genesis 1:2).

The Bible tells us of a loving Father who takes dust and forms a man, who takes a rib and forms a woman. "*God formed man from the dust of the ground, and breathed into his nostrils the breath of life; and man became a living soul*" (Genesis 2:7).

This hands-on act of creation reveals a God who is deeply invested in His creative work and who infuses it with His very breath of life.

We're told of a Father who creates all the natural things we see around us. He created the animals, the trees, the heavens, the earth. Everything we see was made by His hand. "*The Lord God made all kinds of trees grow out of the ground—trees that were pleasing to the eye and good for food*" (Genesis 2:9).

God's creativity is not just functional but also beautiful and enjoyable. He creates with both purpose and pleasure in mind.

The Bible tells us that our Father is the one who formed each of us in our mother's womb. "*For you formed my inmost being. You knit me together in my mother's womb*" (Psalm 139:13).

Your creativity is not an accident or an afterthought - it is a part of who you were made to be, woven into your very being by the Master Creator Himself.

In the New Testament, we see Jesus, the Father personified, living out that same creativity. He changes water into wine, brings life to dead bodies, and brings wholeness to broken bodies.

He takes a handful of loaves and fishes and turns them into a feast for thousands. He told stories that helped to convey truths and ideas that our minds cannot fully comprehend. He was, and is, the light in dark places.

The act of creating is something that reflects His divine nature. As followers of Christ, we are called to be imitators of God (Ephesians 5:1) - and that includes imitating His creativity!

Jesus himself told us that we would do the works he had been doing and even greater things than this. "*Very truly I tell you, whoever believes in me will do the works I have been doing, and they will do even greater things than these, because I am going to the Father*" (John 14:12).

If we believe these words, then we should also believe that the sky is the limit in terms of our potential. The same Spirit that raised Christ from the dead lives in us (Romans 8:11), empowering us to carry on His creative work in the world.

The Bible shows us the creative side of our heavenly Father, through creation and through Jesus' life on earth.

"The Spirit himself testifies with our spirit that we are children of God; and if children, then heirs: heirs of God and joint heirs with Christ" (Romans 8:16-17).

You were imagined in God's mind before the creation of the earth. You're a child of God, adopted into His family.

Your Inheritance

Have you ever seen a TV program like Heir Hunters? They chase down individuals who have been left a legacy from an unclaimed estate. These programs tell stories of individuals who are living in poverty while being completely unaware they stand to inherit life-changing sums.

One man inherited nearly half a million pounds from his long-lost record-collecting recluse of a cousin, thanks to heir hunters. Imagine that!

Maybe up until now, no one's told you about your rights as an heir. Well, today, it's your turn to be the star of the show.

As a child of God, creativity is your heritage - it's your birthright! It's time to claim all that's been given to you, to take possession of your inheritance from your Heavenly Father.

Just as an heir must actively claim their inheritance, we must actively step into our identity as creative beings made in the image of our creative Heavenly Father.

It's time to embrace the truth of who you are and Whose you are. You are not just a creative being - you are called and empowered to reflect God's creativity to the world around you.

So what does this mean for you today? It means it's time to dust off those creative dreams and step out in faith, knowing that the same God who created the stars and billions of galaxies lives in you and wants to create through you.

Your creativity is not mean to be just a hobby or a side hustle - it's part of your sacred calling and part of your kingdom inheritance. Through creativity, we share in God's joy of creating, while expressing His beauty, majesty, and inexpressible wonder to those around us.

So claim your inheritance, step into it, and watch as God uses your unique creative gifts to bring more of His life, light, and love to the world around you.

Your creative adventure with Him is just beginning!

Over To You

What part of your creativity might you have been keeping hidden or overlooking?

……………………………………………………………………………..
……………………………………………………………………………..
……………………………………………………………………………..

What areas of creativity would you like to explore further?

SIX
WHAT IS THE PURPOSE OF CREATIVITY?

As creative children of God, let's turn our attention to the why behind our creativity. Understanding its true purpose will motivate us to push past fear and insecurity to bring our unique gifts to the world.

When did you last have fun, just for the sake of having fun? When did you just play, for the sake of playing? There's a special kind of joy that comes from engaging in activities simply for the pleasure of doing them, without any ulterior motive or goal.

There's a beauty to the happiness of a child absorbed in play, that's clear to any casual observer. Play is something children do effortlessly, but play gets squeezed out of our lives as we grow older. We can see the joy as children play. We intuitively know that their play doesn't have an end goal; it's simply for the joy of the moment.

But we've been taught to believe that play is for children. As adults, our focus is on improving the country's GDP and productivity.

In schools, play is being pushed aside in favour of more *"educational"* activities. In recent years, evidence for the value of play itself has mounted, but we've moved away from play as a goal in itself.

It's not just the education system that's obsessed with outcomes. In our adult world, it seems everything must have a purpose or measurable result to be considered worthwhile. But what if we're missing something vital in this narrow view?

In a world that seeks to quantify everything, what is the outcome of creativity? How can we measure something so intangible? Creating measurable outcomes for our creativity is not only impossible; it goes against the very purpose of creativity.

Measuring Happiness

How do you measure the joy of living purely in the moment, of the way it feels to be in the creative flow? How can you quantify the joy of the creative act and the satisfaction that comes from completion?

How do you express the joy of sensing His presence as you step out in faith? How do you express the satisfaction of being part of God's plan and purpose being lived out, here on the earth?

Society might tell us that there needs to be a purpose or end goal for our creativity. But what if it's the act of getting lost in the "*flow*" state of creativity that is the purpose of creativity? What if the joy we experience as we create is the end goal? What if it's the very act of creativity that is what really matters?

Eric Johnson, from Bethel church, put it like this: "*You are the only one on the face of the earth, in all of time, that can express a certain facet of God.*"

You were born to create - to do as your Heavenly Father did, making something out of nothing. Fulfilling your destiny will bring you more fully into the fullness of life He has promised you.

The Bible talks about the word joy, but "*happiness*" is the word we're more likely to use to express that emotion. We're all searching for our own happiness, in one way or another. Incredibly, researchers have started to explore ways to measure happiness, and the results are surprising.

Some of the most developed nations don't score too well when it comes to "*happiness*." In the World Happiness Report of 2019, the US came 19th, four points below the UK at 15th.

The Australians were rather better at 11th place, and Canada in the top ten at 9th place. Almost every year, the Scandinavian countries of Finland, Denmark, and Norway top the list.

It seems that happiness is elusive, even in some of the most developed nations in the world. When the focus of a nation is on GDP, inflation, and employment, it seems that happiness barely gets a look in. Countries like the Kingdom of Bhutan are leading the way and changing how they measure "*prosperity.*" They've started gauging happiness levels as a measure of prosperity, instead of GDP.

Will we in the so-called developed nations one day discover we've been measuring the wrong things? Will we one day value happiness more than our nation's GDP?

As Mihaly Csikszentmihalyi said, "*For many people, happiness comes from making new things and making discoveries. Enhancing one's creativity may therefore also enhance well-being.*"

Measuring the Immeasurable

Think back to a really positive memory of something which really moved you. It may have been an event or concert you've been to, or something which unexpectedly moved you to tears.

Perhaps it's your favourite musician, a concert, or Christian worship event. Maybe it's a video you watched on social media that caught you off guard with the feelings it evoked.

Have you got a memory in mind? Can you remember the way it made you feel? Imagine trying to express those inner feelings with words. It's almost impossible! You can picture how it made you feel, but it's not so easy to put into words.

We live in a society which is outcome-driven. Words fail to adequately express the value of moments of joy, freedom, or peace.

Expressing the value of creativity is just as elusive. It may not always be tangible or measurable, but it's as real as anything you can hold or see. What if the simple act of creativity, either our own or that of others, brings you happiness?

Of course, creativity is not just about how it makes you feel. It's about living out your highest purpose. As you step out in the creative gifting He's given you, it brings joy to the Father's heart.

Dreams and Visions

It's time to dream a little. To imagine where God might lead you and what God might do through you. To dream of what He might do if you'll follow where He leads.

In Joel 2:28 it promises us, *"It will happen afterward, that I will pour out my Spirit on all flesh; and your sons and your daughters will prophesy. Your old men will dream dreams. Your young men will see visions."*

It's time to ask your Heavenly Father to give you dreams and visions. How do you feel about the idea of God sending you dreams and giving you visions? Maybe you feel a little uncomfortable with or nervous about this idea?

The Bible provides many examples of how God gives people dreams and visions, and equips them to bring those visions to life.

One powerful illustration of this is the story of Bezalel in Exodus 31:1-6, when God called skilled craftsmen to build His temple.

> *I have filled him with the Spirit of God, with wisdom, with understanding, with knowledge and with all kinds of skills—to*

make artistic designs for work in gold, silver and bronze, to cut and set stones, to work in wood, and to engage in all kinds of crafts.

God also appointed Oholiab and other skilled workers to help Bezalel construct this sacred space, saying, *"Also I have given ability to all the skilled workers to make everything I have commanded you."*

We see that when God gives someone a vision of what they are to create, He also provides the skills needed to bring it to life.

Just as He filled Bezel with His Spirit, He wants to fill you with His spirit and equip you to carry out the dreams He's laid on your heart.

We also see that, in His hands, our creativity, is a form of worship and service to Him. Our creativity has a sacred purpose.

In a society which focuses on our jobs or achievements, having a dream is in danger of becoming something negative. It bucks the trend, goes against the so-called norm.

In every age, dreamers have sometimes been viewed with skepticism, sometimes even in the church. It's only in retrospect that we acclaim them as visionaries and applaud their achievements.

As the artist Van Gogh said, "*I can't change the fact that my paintings don't sell. But the time will come when people will recognise that they are worth more than the value of the paints used in the picture.*" Van Gogh died penniless at the age of 37.

Maybe in the past you've been told that your dreams are just that, "*dreams*." You've been told that you need to grow up, settle down, and stop dreaming. Yet dreams and visions are seen regularly right through the Bible. And it's easy to forget what the history books tell us.

Some of the greatest discoveries have been made because someone was having fun playing with an idea. Imagine a world without Berners-Lee's internet, or a world without Alexander Fleming's penicillin. Or a world poorer for not having the riches of Howard Carter's Tutankhamun.

Imagine a world without Edison's light bulb, or a world without da Vinci's Mona Lisa. Or a world without C.S. Lewis's The Lion, The Witch and the Wardrobe, Roald Dahl's Charlie and the Chocolate Factory, or J.K. Rowling's Harry Potter.

Imagine a world without Einstein's Theory of Relativity or the planes of the Wright brothers. Or even a world without the music of Elvis, Michael Jackson, or the Beatles.

Some of the greatest creations in today's world have come about because someone dared to pursue a seemingly impossible dream.

As Harriet Tubman said, "*Every great dream begins with a dreamer. Always remember, you have within you the strength, the patience, and the passion to reach for the stars to change the world.*"

Or as Eleanor Roosevelt put it, "*The future belongs to those who believe in the beauty of their dreams.*" The Bible is full of men and women who had visions and dreamed dreams.

Jacob dreamt of angels ascending and descending. Sarah had long since given up on her dream of motherhood, yet God spoke to her and visited her, and she became pregnant. Joseph dreamed that one day his older brothers would bow before him.

"Look up into the sky and count the stars if you can. That's how many descendants you will have!" (Genesis 15:5) Abraham chose to believe God when He promised that Abraham would have as many offspring as the stars in the sky.

Jesus's father, Joseph, was warned in a dream to flee from Bethlehem to Egypt with Mary and Jesus. Deborah was a prophet and judge who heard from God, spoke to Barak, which brought about a mighty victory for the Israelite army.

The Lord spoke to Ananias in a vision, telling him to go lay hands on the eyes of a man named Saul, who would become the Apostle Paul.

Paul had also been given a vision that a man named Ananias would come and lay hands on his blinded eyes. Peter had a vision of a sheet of animals, showing him that God was welcoming the Gentiles into His family.

What's Your Dream?

The Bible says that God wants to give you the desires of your heart. *"Delight yourself in Yahweh, and he will give you the desires of your heart."* (Psalm 37:4) He not only created you, but He's placed desires in your heart that He longs to fulfil!

He hasn't put your desires there to frustrate you or make you feel discouraged. He's put desires in your heart to move you out of your comfort zones. As you delight yourself in Him, He wants to give you what you yearn for.

As Martin Luther said, *"The Christian shoemaker does his duty not by putting little crosses on the shoes, but by making good shoes, because God is interested in good craftsmanship."*

He wants to challenge you to reach for dreams that He'll place in your heart. As you do so, you'll reflect something of His glory to the world around you.

There's something that only you can bring to the world.

As you dare to dream, who knows what God will do?

Over To You

Think of something that's been created (for example, a book, movie or music) that you have enjoyed recently

....

....

....

Did any of the words about creativity resonate with you or stir your heart? If so, which ones?

....

....

....

If you could 'play' at creativity, just for fun, what would you like to have a go at?

....

....

....

Reflect for a moment. When have you created something that didn't previously exist? Do you think others might consider your actions as creative?

....

....

....

SEVEN
WHAT'S YOUR DREAM?

Throughout history, God has used ordinary men and women who dared to dream big and believe that He could do the extraordinary through them.

In this chapter, we'll look at some of these inspiring examples, from the pages of the Bible to more recent times. We'll see how God took small seeds of faith and transformed them into extraordinary movements that impacted countless lives.

As we look at their journeys of faith and courage, I encourage you to start opening your heart and mind to what God might want to do through you.

What passions has He placed within you? What needs stir your heart to action? It's time to dream big, take risks, and trust God to do immeasurably more than you can imagine!

But before we go further, let's address something that often holds us back …

Comparison : The Killer of Dreams

Do you ever feel tempted to compare yourself with other Christian women? It's something that most of us seem to struggle with, at one time or another.

When you play the comparison game, you can feel as if you don't measure up. You might even discount yourself from God's purposes because you're not at all like them.

But you're not called to be like them. Your Heavenly Father made you just as you are for a reason.

You're not called to fulfil their dreams, you're called to fulfil yours!

Let me share a story of someone who refused to let comparison with those far more gifted than her stop her from following the dream God gave her.

A young woman felt called to overseas missions. She tried every door possible.

The missions agencies she spoke with told her she wasn't qualified, saying she didn't have what it took to be a missionary.

Yet she couldn't deny the calling she felt in her heart.

She was so convinced that she'd heard from God that, despite everyone telling her she wasn't the right person, she used her life savings to buy a train ticket and began her journey.

The rest of her story is history, the stuff of legends.

You may have heard of her, her name was Gladys Aylward.

Gladys was a missionary to China who impacted the nation for God.

Gladys had a dream that God could use one woman to impact a nation. Here's what she said about herself:

> *"I wasn't God's first choice for what I've done in China, I don't know who it was, it must've been a man, a well educated man.*
>
> *I don't know what happened, perhaps he died, perhaps he wasn't willing? And God looked down and saw Gladys Aylward and God said well she's willing."*

Despite what the so-called missionary experts said about her, Gladys impacted many in China for Christ. By taking one simple step at a time, knowing that God was leading her, she changed many lives.

This pattern of ordinary people doing extraordinary things through faith runs throughout Scripture and history. Like Gladys, countless men and women throughout history have stepped out in faith to pursue what must have seemed impossible to others. They remind us that when God gives us a dream, He also gives us the courage to pursue it.

If we look at the lives of these men and women from the Bible and from history, we find a common thread. Each of them followed their own path, believed the impossible or believed for breakthroughs that others thought impossible.

Nehemiah had a dream to restore the city of Jerusalem.

Gideon believed God could use him to defeat an army of thousands with just 300 men.

David believed he could defeat a giant that had terrified an entire army.

Elizabeth had a dream that she could one day be a mother.

Hannah persisted in prayer and saw her dream of having a son she could dedicate to God fulfilled.

Dorcas dreamed of using her creative skills in sewing to help others, believing she could make a difference through practical creativity.

Lydia used her business skills and believed God could use her home and resources to establish one of the first churches in Europe.

The Wright brothers had a dream to fly.

Marie Curie had a dream to one day become a scientist.

Hudson Taylor had a dream to see China changed for God.

Jim and Elisabeth Elliot had a dream to share Christ with an unreached people group.

William Wilberforce dreamed of ending the slave trade.

Amy Carmichael dreamed of rescuing children from temple prostitution in India.

George Müller dreamed of caring for thousands of orphans through faith alone.

Corrie ten Boom dreamed of helping as many Jewish people as possible escape the Holocaust.

Jackie Pullinger dreamed of bringing hope to the Walled City of Hong Kong.

Brother Andrew dreamed of smuggling Bibles behind the Iron Curtain.

Each of these men and women faced fears and challenges, yet their faith helped them overcome these seemingly insurmountable obstacles.

They remind us that God-given dreams have the power to change lives and even nations. Their stories challenge us to ask: what dreams has God planted in your heart? And more importantly, what will you do with those dreams?

While we may not all be called to change nations or make history, we are called to impact our family, our workplace, our neighbours and our local community. What matters isn't the size of your impact, but your faithfulness to use what God has given you.

What you do with your life matters.

Inside each of us, God has placed seeds of creativity. We're made in His likeness. Creativity is in our very DNA.

When you follow the desires He has placed in your heart, you will be stepping into a life filled with meaning and purpose.

Of course, it's all too easy to let your God-given gifts sit gathering dust, or to bury them. It's far easier to stay within your comfort zone. Yet your comfort zone is not where you'll see your dreams fulfilled and God break in.

You can choose to explore your full potential or you can choose to ignore it.

As a child of the King, you're called to live an exceptional life. To nurture your dreams, to run with the vision He's given you.

Your heavenly Father delights in giving good gifts to His children. As James 1:17 reminds us, *"Every good and perfect gift is from above, coming down from the Father of the heavenly lights."*

As His child, you can be confident that He's given you talents, even if you're as yet unsure how or where to use them.

Think about this for a moment:

What if Gladys Aylward had refused to follow her dream?

What if Esther hadn't believed that God could do something with her life?

What if Rahab had discounted herself because of the life she led?

Each of these women could have let fear steal their dream. Instead, they chose to step out in faith. As Hebrews 12 1-2 tells us *"let us run with endurance the race that is set before us, looking to Jesus the founder and perfecter of our faith."*

There's a race He wants you to run. It's up to you to discover what that race is, and to run it with all your heart.

Like those who've gone before you, step forward with expectancy.

You should feel as excited as a child on Christmas morning, eager to unwrap and enjoy all that He has given you.

What's Your Dream?

Stop for a moment. Close your eyes and open your mind.

What problems do you see around you that need fixing? What do you get on your soap box about? What's on your heart to do or change? Maybe there's something you've just had this nagging feeling about - you just know that someone, somewhere ought to do something about it.

However small, what is it on your heart to do? What is it that you have a passion to do or see changed?

Finally, what is the one thing you would do if you knew you couldn't fail? Think of all the things you love to do, make or create. Think of those long-buried dreams. Remember the vision that God has given you. Allow yourself to dream.

Why Me?

It's okay to ask the question, 'who am I' that God would choose to use me? Many of the people we meet in the pages of our Bibles asked just that same question.

Mary asked that question when told she would carry the saviour of the world. Moses asked that question when God called him to lead a nation.

We're broken people living in a messed up world. This world is vast, far bigger than we can imagine. By comparison, we can feel small or insignificant.

Yet our Heavenly Father sees things differently. He doesn't see us as small or insignificant. He sees us as sons and daughters of the King.

He sees this messed-up world and calls each one of us to play our part, to make a difference. He chose us to reflect something of his glorious nature to those around us.

We reflect Him when we create beauty, when we share love, or stand up for truth. We're called to make a difference in our small corner of the world. But, how do we do this when we feel so weak and insignificant?

God's Promises to You

Let's take a look at some Bible verses which you're probably familiar with. They speak of God's promises to you and of your identity as His child.

Take a moment to listen, open your heart and receive these promises from your Heavenly Father:

"My grace is sufficient for you, for my power is made perfect in weakness." (2 Corinthians 12:9)

"But you will receive power when the Holy Spirit comes upon you." (Acts 1:8)

"Do you not know that you are a temple of God and that the Spirit of God dwells in you?" (1 Corinthians 3:16)

God has promised to give you what you need, when you need it. He's placed His Holy Spirit inside you. He promises that you can do all things through Christ who gives you strength (Phil 4:13). He calls you to "*be strong in the Lord and in His mighty power.*" (Ephesians 6:10)

These aren't just nice words to read - they're God's promises to you. The God who created everything lives inside you! He's right there with you, giving you strength for each step. When this truth sinks in, those impossible dreams don't seem quite so impossible anymore.

Now, armed with these promises, it's time to dream!

Dare to Dream

Thousands of lives have been changed because people just like you dared to dream.

As Julia Cameron, author of The Artist's Way, observed:

> *"When we survey our lives, seeking to fulfil our creativity, we often see we had a dream that went glimmering because we believed, and those around us believed, that the dream was beyond our reach. Many of us would have been, or at least might have been, done, tried something, if...If we had known who we really were."*

Perhaps, like Cameron, you once had a dream that faded away because you thought it was beyond your reach or abilities.

The artist Henri Matisse once said, "*Creativity takes courage.*" Just as every artist must face a blank canvas, we too must courageously step into the possibilities God places before us.

You may have been hurt in the past by daring to dream. Will you take a risk and dare to dream again? Will you allow yourself to be moulded and shaped in the hands of your loving heavenly Father? Will you dare to believe that God is bigger than your fears and failures?

Listen closely. Can you hear him saying it's time? It's time to explore your God-given gifts and creativity. Time to listen to His voice. Time to conquer your fears. Time to step out in courage and faith.

Still Waiting?

If you don't feel God has given you a dream or is calling you to something, that's OK. Maybe for you, allowing yourself to dream or listen to God is the first step in your journey. If that's you, you might find the next chapter helpful, as it's all about learning to listen to hear His voice.

But never forget - you have the indwelling presence and power of your Heavenly Father living inside you. The same Spirit that raised Christ from the dead lives in you. God is bigger than all of your fears. His grace is sufficient. His strength is greater than your weakness.

Whether your dream is clear or still taking shape, one thing is certain: you were created with purpose. Each day is an opportunity to step out and discover what God might do through you.

So perhaps it's time to stop asking "*why me?*" and start asking "*what next?*"

Over To You

What problems do you see around you that need fixing? What do you get on your soap box about? If you're not sure, ask your friends and family!

....
....
....

Is there something on your heart to create, make, do or change? What's your dream?

....
....
....

What fears have been holding you back from taking the first small step towards your creative dreams?

....
....
....

EIGHT
HEARING GOD'S WHISPER

Do you long to hear God's voice more clearly in your life? To receive His wisdom, direction, and comfort right when you need it most?

If so, you're not alone.

Across the ages, God has spoken to all kinds of men and women, and He wants to speak to you today.

He longs to give you spiritual insight and wisdom, direction and comfort, all of which can come as you listen for His voice.

In the busyness and chaos of life, it's not always easy to discern God's voice. But the good news is that hearing from God is a skill we can grow in, just like any other.

In this chapter, we'll explore practical ways to cultivate a listening ear and learn to recognise when God is speaking to us.

We'll tackle some of the common fears and doubts that hold us back, and be inspired by examples of how God uses ordinary people who are willing to listen and obey.

We'll also look at what the Bible teaches about hearing from God and how we can apply this to our lives.

Get ready to embark on the most important adventure of your life - learning to hear from the God who loves you more than you can imagine!

Hearing God

It's not always easy to hear God in this busy world.

When we call to Him, our Heavenly Father promises to reveal great things to us. *"Call to me and I will answer you, and I will tell you great and hidden things that you have not known."* (Jeremiah 33:3) He promises that He will answer you when you cry out to him.

Hearing from God, can help us make it through the toughest of times. His voice can help to lead us, when we feel lost and it can empower us to become the world-changers He created us to be.

But how do we learn to hear and discern His voice, in the midst of our busy and chaotic lives?

It's hard enough to listen to anyone, let along God. So, how do we do this in the midst of constant busyness?

We can start by taking time to quiet ourselves and listen for His still, small voice.

Listening for His voice begins the moment we choose to follow Him. It can happen when we choose to obey when we think we hear his voice.

Something beautiful happens in our relationship with our heavenly Father when He sees we are willing to trust Him. As Bill Hybels reminds us in his book "Power of a Whisper," *"God's desire to communicate with His people is woven throughout Scripture and continues today"*.

From Adam and Eve walking in the garden to the apostle John receiving revelations on Patmos, the Bible illustrates God's unchanging desire to speak with His people.

And God hasn't changed - He still hears and speaks to us today!

Changing Your Perspective

To understand how God speaks to us, we must first understand who He is.

In our self-focused world, it's all too easy for us to want to bring Him down to our size. It's time for us to have a far bigger view of God. To truly see Him as He is, we need to get a sense of perspective.

Stop for a moment and think about our amazing God. He is the creator of the universe, the creator of everything you see around you.

Your God is impossibly enormous, bigger than you can even conceive or think. He is the Alpha and Omega. He is the beginning and the end. He created all things and in Him all things hold together.

The same hands that set the stars in place are the hands that formed you. He holds this world in His hands and He holds you in His hands.

Have you ever seen a mountain or something enormous in the distance? Did it seem even larger than you imagined, as you got closer? Maybe you've seen something that's taken your breath away, with its majesty or beauty? This is just a glimpse of His greatness.

Who are we to think we could stop the God of the universe from speaking when He chooses?

No matter who you are or what you've done, you are His beloved child and He wants to talk to you.

And on those days when you doubt this, just remind yourself that, if God can speak through a donkey (Numbers 22:28), then He can speak to you!

Overcoming Our Barriers

Even if we believe that God wants to speak to us, we can often face mental hurdles to overcome.

Sometimes the thought of hearing from God can make us feel anxious. We wonder if we'll hear Him when He is speaking to us. But hearing from God isn't just something that happens—it's part of the journey we're on and something we can grow in.

King David spent years tending sheep on the hillside learning to recognise God's voice. Moses had to overcome his own insecurities and fears before he could lead God's people out of Egypt.

If God could speak to and use them, He can use you too. Remember, it's not about your ability, it's about His ability.

It's natural to wonder if you're able to hear from God. Change your perspective for a moment, and remember that if God wants to speak to you (and the Bible clearly says that He does), then who are you to stop Him? God's ability to speak is far greater than your inability to hear.

Ephesians 3:20 tells us that God is able to do far more than we can ask or imagine, according to His power at work within us. His resurrection power is living inside you!

Despite your failures, despite your weakness, the God of the universe wants to speak to you. He's placed His Holy Spirit power inside of you. His longing is to walk with you and give you the courage you need. All you need to do is still yourself and listen.

The Psalmist David captures this beautifully: *"At the very moment I called out to you, you answered me! You strengthened me deep within my soul and breathed fresh courage into me."* (Psalm 138:3 TPT).

This promise shows when we feel weak and fearful - He is ready to breathe courage into us. He doesn't just listen, He give us strength and courage.

In Psalm 73:24, we find further reassurance, *"You hold me by my right hand, you lead me with your secret wisdom."* We can be confident that we are not walking this path alone, He is walking with us, holding our hand and giving us the wisdom we need for each and every situation.

Grasping the truth - that His ability to speak to you is so much greater than your inability to hear—can transform your life. Why do you think that God can't use you? Is your weakness really bigger than God's strength?

It's time to get out of the way and let God flow in and through your life. Put down any preconceived ideas, and let go of your pride. Follow where He leads and make a commitment to follow Him, whatever the cost.

Perhaps the cost will be stepping out in faith, when you'd rather hide in the shadows. Maybe the cost will be to your pride, as you let go of placing importance on what people think of you and choose to ask your Heavenly Father what He says about you.

Whatever barriers you need to remove, whatever you need to overcome, once you start hearing His voice regularly, I believe you will believe that it was worth it.

Starting Small: The First Steps

Once we understand who God is and have addressed our barriers, how do we begin this journey of hearing His voice?

I believe that we need to start to hear God in the small things. Here's something of my own journey.

Early in my Christian walk, I wanted to hear from God, but I wasn't sure how to get started. As I read my Bible, I could see people hearing from God, with such clear direction. I felt anxious about getting it wrong, of heading off in the wrong direction.

Someone shared this story with me, which I find encouraging to this day: A woman thinks she's heard from God. She follows the voice she thinks she's heard.

God is sat on the sidelines, cheering her on. "*Look,*" He says, "*see what she does when they think they've heard from me? I can't wait to see what she'll do when she really hears from me.*"

God delights in our small steps of faith, even when we're not totally sure it's Him speaking. He is patient with us as we learn to recognize His voice.

At the start of my journey, hearing from God seemed almost impossible. I didn't know where to start. I'd heard the Biblical principle that if you're faithful in the small things, God will reward you with more.

As a busy mum with three children under the age of 5, that idea really struck a chord with me. Life was busy, but my contribution seemed small and insignificant. I longed for greater meaning outside the home but didn't see how I could squeeze more into my busy days.

One day a magazine advert caught my attention. A prisoner on death row in Trinidad and Tobago was looking for someone to write letters to him as a penpal. I went to bed that night with thoughts of that prisoner in my head. Waking, I realised that during the spare moments of my day, I could find the time to write a letter.

As I sat down in front of that blank page, I honestly didn't know what to write. The British are known for talking about the weather, holidays, cars, sport or food. These weren't the sort of things it seemed right to write about with someone facing execution.

It was time for my next step in my journey in listening to God. Each time I sat down to write a letter, I asked my Heavenly Father to put something on my heart to share. Whatever was brought to mind, I'd share, trusting that He was leading and helping me.

There were no blinding lights to guide me, just a sense of trusting that what God had laid on my heart would be what he needed to hear. I had to step out in faith, believing that God would guide my words, even when I felt uncertain or not up to the task.

Like the widow offering her two small coins (Luke 21:1-4), I had to trust that God could use my seemingly insignificant offering to somehow make a difference.

I soon found myself writing to a number of prisoners across the world, through the organisation Prisoners Abroad.

Every time I sat down to write a letter, and looked at that blank page, I'd have to lean in and listen for that gentle whisper. As I sat down to write, I found myself so encouraged, especially as I reflected on how even the simple pleasures in life that we so often take for granted could bring hope to others.

In the same way as I'd been leaning into his voice, trusting Him to speak, I began to trust Him to use me to speak to those around me. At first, was just a single word. Then a sentence. My journey started with such small things, yet has continued to grow and change me as I lean in to listen for His voice.

Your journey of hearing God's voice can begin just as simply.

Start with those quiet moments, those small promptings, and trust that He will meet you there.

As you practice listening in the everyday moments of life, you'll find His voice becoming clearer and your confidence growing.

Don't despise the day of small beginnings (Zechariah 4:10). Be faithful with the small things and God will entrust you with more.

Remember, every great journey begins with a single step – and God is ready to walk beside you, speaking to your heart, every step of the way.

Moving Beyond Listening

Have you ever had the experience of asking someone to do something, yet they didn't do what you asked?

Maybe you even asked them about it and they replied, "*Yes, I heard you.*" It's so annoying when that happens, isn't it?

Yet sometimes we're a little like that with God.

Listening really is only the first step. The next step is rather more challenging. It's not good enough to merely listen to the word, we need to do what it says (James 1:22). So, when we hear God's voice, we need to respond.

Now that you've heard from God, it's time to respond in faith and act on what you hear. This is the point at which we stop looking at Jesus in wonder and we start to really follow Him.

In a world where following our own will and desires is given so much importance, this is definitely a counter-cultural calling. He called His disciples to leave their nets and follow Him. Their nets were all they had to earn their livelihood, and yet Jesus called them to put them down to follow Him.

He promises to speak to us through His Holy Spirit, residing inside us. He promises that when we call He will answer.

Hearing God's voice is not the hardest thing—the hardest thing for us can be to obey and follow the voice we hear.

But as we step out in faith and obedience, even when it's costly or uncomfortable, we will start to experience and know the abundant life Jesus promised in John 10:10.

When we disobey, or fail to act on what we've heard, that still, small voice will grow quieter or even become silent.

When we obey (John 14:23), even when it's not easy, we open ourselves up to the joy of hearing from Him more.

The Journey Forward

What does this mean for our ongoing walk with Him?

Maybe you dream of a life where you're led by Him, hear from Him each step of the way. Maybe that's the life you used to have, but something happened along the way, and that life of living close to God seems far away.

Can you remember a time when you felt you heard from God? A time when you followed His leading? Perhaps a time when He spoke and you hesitated or even dismissed it?

There's no condemnation here. It's important to be honest about where you're at, to empower you to move forward. One of the reasons that we don't seem to hear from God is that we hesitate or refuse to follow where He leads.

It can be all too easy to discount ourselves, thinking we're unworthy, weak or to fear failure.

It's OK to fear failure. Sometimes you will get it wrong. But you'll also get it gloriously right sometimes too!

We all fail. That's part and parcel of our normal life.

What makes a great man or woman of God isn't their failures. What makes them great is acknowledging that failure and turning to God, asking Him for the strength and courage to follow where He leads.

For the men and women we meet in the pages of our Bible, this wasn't always their experience either. Many of them had a moment where they failed to trust where God was leading them.

Think about Moses, Abraham, and Jonah. Each of them had to come humbly to God. Each of them had to repent and turn from their old ways. They learned a new and different way, a way of trusting and acting when they heard God's voice.

Oftentimes they didn't understand. Yet, they followed.

We're reminded in Proverbs 3:5-6 (NLT) to *"Trust in the Lord with all your heart; do not depend on your own understanding. Seek his will in all you do, and he will show you which path to take."*

That's His promise to us—that if we trust Him, even when we don't fully understand the picture, He will show us the way.

It's the same for us too. We need to come humbly to our Heavenly Father. We need to repent, turning from our old ways and learn a new and different way. We need to grow in trust and act when we hear God's voice, even if we don't fully understand.

A Prayer

Let's take a moment to respond to God in prayer.

Father, thank you for your gift of life.

Thank you that you love me, and you know everything about me.

I long to hear you speaking to me. I long to hear your voice.

I want to follow You and know Your voice each step of my way.

I want you to guide and direct my path.

Yet, I know that sometimes I've messed up and got things wrong.

I want to say that I'm sorry.

I'm sorry for the times when I've heard your voice and failed to follow through.

I'm sorry for the times when it's been too difficult or costly to follow you.

I'm sorry for those times when I felt weak and failed to trust Your voice.

Forgive me for the times when I've gone my own way.

Forgive me for those times when I've not had the courage to follow You.

I ask for Your forgiveness and for the joy of hearing Your voice again.

Please give me the courage to follow you with my whole heart, to follow and not turn back.

When I feel weak, help me to trust You to speak.

Help me to trust Your still small voice, to obey and follow You.

Father, you are the One who speaks the words of eternal life.

Today, I choose to trust You. I choose to follow You, wherever You may lead.

Over To You

In what ways does God most often speak to you?

....

....

....

Reflect on a time when you sensed God speaking to you. What was that experience like? How did you respond?

....
....
....

What fears or doubts do you have about hearing from God? How might you hand these over to Him?

....
....
....

NINE
FEAR: THE ENEMY OF CREATIVITY

Are you letting fear hold you back from embracing your God-given creativity? Are you allowing that spark of divine inspiration to be quenched?

If we're honest with ourselves, most of us are living with some level of fear and anxiety, whether we realise it or not.

Fear has become so deeply woven into the fabric of our daily lives that we often don't even recognise how much it controls us.

Imagine living in hiding for 32 years, seeing no-one but a close family member. That's the haunting and true story of Janez Ruz, a young shoemaker who fully supported the Nazi regime during the Second World War.

When the Nazis fell from power, Janez feared retribution and fled to his sister's home in Slovenia. For over three decades, he hid himself away in a barn on her farm, never seeing anyone other than his sister.

When discovered, Janez told reporters that he'd wasted more than thirty years of his life.

Janez allowed fear to rob him of a full life. How many of us, like Janez, are letting fear hold us back from truly living?

But here's the good news: we don't have to stay stuck in fear. Throughout the Bible, we see countless examples of men and women who faced their fears head-on and chose to step out in faith and obedience to God's call.

In this chapter, we'll explore what it means to live from a place of faith rather than fear. We'll examine some practical steps you can take to identify and overcome the fears that are holding you back.

Get ready to discover how conquer your fears and step into the abundant, creative life God has for you!

Understanding Fear

Living with fear has become so normal to us, that we simply cannot see it anymore. It seems as if everyone lives with fear.

Adam Smith (in his book "The Bravest You: 5 Steps to Fight Your Biggest Fears, Find Your Passion and Unlock Your Extraordinary Life") reminds us that, *"Fear is the number one obstacle you will face in life. The most difficult challenge you will ever be put to and the most important one to overcome."*

Most of our lives are controlled, to some degree at least, by our fears.

As Elizabeth Gilbert, author of *Eat, Pray, Love*, puts it:

> *If you can just release yourself from the anxiety and burden that might be associated with the word 'creativity,' you'll see, in fact, that you are an enormously creative person.**

The reality is that every day of our lives, without even being aware of it, most of us are living with fear.

Yet, it's only as we release ourselves from our fears and anxieties, that we can start to embrace the creativity inside of us.

Fear In Our Lives

Perhaps you don't feel as if your life is ruled by fear? Then let me ask you a simple question. Is your life free from anxiety?

Stop for a moment and honestly consider what you've been feeling anxious about lately.

What worries run through your mind through your day or keep you awake at night? What thoughts fill your mind as you go through your day?

We tell ourselves that everyone experiences anxiety. We're used to feeling anxiety, because it seems so normal, even necessary.

Whether you call it worry or anxiety, at the root of both is fear. And fear is a monster, a monster that can ruin lives, if we allow it to.

---

* https://www.inc.com/jessica-stillman/3-mind-blowing-truths-about-creativity.html

Fear can hold us back from a life of faith. Fear can prevent us from living the lives of joy, fulfilment and freedom that God desires for us. But it was never meant to be that way.

The Bible speaks of one fear that conquers all fears. It tells us that '*it is for freedom, that Christ has set us free*' (Galatians 5:1).

Elsewhere we read that '*If the son sets you free, you will be free indeed.*' (John 8:36)

We're supposed to know and live in freedom, yet we're consumed by anxiety. Jesus came to destroy these enemies of our soul once and for all. So, why are our lives ruled by anxiety and fear?

Why do so few of us experience the joy and freedom that is our inheritance?

Fear vs Faith

It's important to distinguish between healthy and unhealthy fears. Not all fear is bad. The right fears can keep us safe.

Fear has a place in our lives.

We fear touching something hot because it might burn us. We fear stepping out into moving traffic, because moving cars can kill or injure us.

While healthy fears such as these clearly serve a purpose, unfortunately all too often Christians are held back by unhealthy fears, especially when it comes to their God-given creativity.

Unhealthy fears don't keep us safe but instead hold us back. These include fear of failure, rejection, change, uncertainty, or what others may think or say about us. They can imprison us and keep us from living the lives God intended for us.

Jesus illustrated this in the parable of the talents (Matthew 25:14-30). He told a story of three servants given different amounts of money, or talents. Two took risks and doubled their masters investment.

One man, paralysed with fear, buried the talent in the ground. It was this man who buried his talent, who allowed fear to rule, that Jesus was displeased with.

The message is clear: it doesn't matter what your talent is, what your gifts are, whether they're more or less than those around you. What matters is that you don't allow fear to keep you from using whatever gifts God has given you.

The reality is that many Christians allow fear, rather than faith, to rule their lives.

Perhaps you're shaking your head at this point, thinking that this is not you. Then let me ask you, have you ever hesitated to use your creative gifts to serve others or glorify God?

Or perhaps you create in the comfort of your own home, but never share your work with others? Maybe you self-censor or limit your creative expression, to that which others can understand or will approve?

If any of this sounds familiar, you're not alone. Fear is a common struggle for many of us, especially when it comes to our creativity.

Brené Brown reminds us, *"Creativity is the way I share my soul with the world."*

When we allow fear to hold us back from creating or sharing our work, we limit our ability to share our soul and connect authentically with others.

When we allow fear to control us, instead of being motivated by faith, our creative journey suffers. We hesitate to use our God-given gifts, pulling back from taking steps of faith in our creative pursuits.

Too often, we settle for safe, unremarkable work instead of pursuing the innovative and impactful creativity God has called us to. Most painfully, we hide our creative talents instead of sharing them with others.

When our fears hold us back, something precious slips away.

Take a moment to reflect - which of these patterns feels most familiar? Perhaps you recognise yourself, remembering times when fear held you back from sharing your gifts?

Have you sometimes felt a prompting to do something creative, but held back, because you're afraid of what others may say?

Perhaps you've felt God lead you to do something new or innovative, but have feared that you're not up to the challenge, or that your gifts aren't 'good' enough?

Instead of living lives characterised by faith and courage, we live lives characterised by compromise and anxiety.

Instead of taking the bold steps of faith God calls us to, we live small, safe lives, afraid of stepping outside of our small, safe worlds.

We choose to be safe and unremarkable, rather than bold world-changers. We choose to live in the shadows, rather than stepping out into the light.

As Theresa Dedmon (author of Born to Create) states, "*If we want to fully access God's limitless creativity, we must be willing to venture into the waves of risk and uncertainty.*"

Just stop for a moment and think about a time when you think God may have spoken to you, but you didn't follow through. We've all been there at some point in our lives. That moment doesn't define you. How you respond to it is what will define you.

Do you remember what Gladys Aylward said about her calling? She believed that God had called a well-educated man, who perhaps wasn't willing to follow God to China.

Jonah's story illustrates this - he tried to run from God's call on his life, and that didn't work out so well for him. The wrong fears don't keep us safe; they quench the fire of faith.

As Christian creatives, we face unique challenges when it comes to fear. We have to overcome our fear of rejection or criticism from others who may not understand or appreciate our creative work.

We need to learn to rely on the Holy Spirit to empower and lead us, and to trust His guidance, rather than leaning on our own wisdom.

When success or compliments come our way, we need to step aside, and point people to the Creator, who inspires our work.

The Impact of Fear on Creativity

Creativity is an expression of freedom.

To flourish, a society needs its artists and creatives, to bring their creativity into the world.

If you look back through history, whenever a restrictive regime takes control, it's often the creatives and intellectuals that are imprisoned or eliminated.

As actress Stella Adler once said, *"Life beats down and crushes the soul and art reminds you that you have one."*

Creativity is a powerful force for change and progress. It can challenge the status quo, provoke thought, and inspire new ideas. This is why oppressive regimes fear and target creatives – because art and creativity have the power to open minds and hearts.

But fear can stifle our creativity and keep us from taking risks. Fear can kill our ability to dream and take risks, our desire to shoot for the stars and it robs us of joy. Fear can limit our ability to take risks, to get it wrong or to look foolish.

This is exactly what Joseph Chilton Pearce meant when he said, "to *live a creative life, we must lose our fear of being wrong."*

Being willing to take risks or get it wrong takes courage, so let's take a look at what the Bible tells us about having courage.

Noah faced derision for what seems like a hare-brained plot to build a boat in the middle of nowhere. Nehemiah was laughed at because of his plan to rebuild the walls of

Jerusalem. Esther had to overcome her fears, to break with tradition and approach the king unbidden.

It takes courage to face our fears. It's normal to experience fear. It's okay to feel fearful or anxious, but it's what we do about our feelings that defines us. It's what we do with our fear that determines our trajectory.

It's easy to feel that fear is in control of us, yet this is not the truth. We can control how we respond to fear. We can choose to act in faith, rather than to live in fear.

An old Cherokee story illustrates this point well.

A grandfather sat down to talk with his grandson.
"There are two wolves inside each of us.
One of these wolves is anger, hate, greed and pride, the other wolf is joy, love, kindness and generosity.
This fight is going on inside of every person."

His grandson thought a while, then asked the question,
"Grandfather, which wolf will win?"
His grandfather replied, "The one you feed."

Just as in this story, you are not subject to all those feelings rising up inside you. You have a choice. You can choose to feed yourself with the right things, to focus on what is good, and change the outcome.

We can trust in the one who holds everything in his hands. We can trust him because he will either calm the storm, or calm our hearts as we live through the storm.

With creativity our greatest fears can be that we are simply deluding ourselves, that we have no creativity inside of us, that we are merely imposters, and will one day be found out as such.

When this kind of fear arises, there is only one place to return to. That is the place where you can hear the still small voice of God speaking to your heart, leading and guiding you.

For, wherever he leads, we must follow, whatever the cost. So count the cost. Those closest to you may not understand.

Fear also keeps us trapped in perfectionism and comparison. We live in an age where it's all too easy to compare ourselves to others and come up short.

We live in a society where it's easy to see or experience the very best of anything.

You can quickly Google and find amazing photographers, fabulous chefs or talented artists.

As little as 100 years ago, if you were good at your craft, you would have been acknowledged and valued by your local community.

Now, both you and those around you are comparing your creativity with the very best of the best, and often you may feel that you come up short.

Think how easy it is today to listen to the best preachers in the world and compare your own preacher's efforts on Sunday.

Or how easy it is to compare your life with the lives you see on social media.

It's no wonder that we can feel paralysed into inaction.

In a society which prizes the intellect and achievement, you may wonder if there really is a place for creativity.

Despite the challenges we face today, creativity has been valued throughout history. If we look back through history, the answer is an unequivocal 'yes!' Down through the ages, art has been valued for art's sake.

In much of Europe, the skill of the Artisan is highly valued. As you drive through France, you'll see signs for artisans of all kinds - from bread bakers to cabinet makers.

Our current low view of the creative act is just a blip in history, one that I believe will correct itself in time.

Choosing Faith Over Fear

Fear is one of the greatest enemies we face, but we don't have to let fear win. We have a choice.

We can feed our faith, trust in the Creator, who has gifted us with creativity for a purpose.

Our path won't always be easy. There will be times when our fear seems easier to hear than the still, small voice of God.

But, every time we choose to step out in faith, every time you choose to create, to share your creations with the world, you are pushing back the darkness, one act of courage at a time.

The Psalmist offers hope for those walking through challenging seasons: *"We've passed through fire and flood, yet in the end you always bring us out better than we were before"* (Psalm 67:12 NLT).

This promise reminds us that our creative journey isn't about avoiding fear or difficulty, but about trusting that God can transform our challenges to bring us out better than we were before.

So, what one small step of creative courage can you take today? How can you step out in some small way, to embrace the creative seeds that God has planted within you?

Whatever you choose, remember, the Creator Himself is cheering you on, every step of the way.

Over To You

What specific fears tend to hold you back from living out your God-given creativity?

....

....

....

Which biblical characters do you most relate to in facing fears? What can you learn from their example?

....

....

....

TEN
BREAKING THROUGH CREATIVE BARRIERS

Biblical Examples of Overcoming Fear

The Bible is full of men and women who came face to face with fear but chose to allow their faith to lead them.

Let's take a look at some of those stories:

Esther faced up to her fears. When she went before her husband the King to plead for her people, she knew he could condemn her to death in a moment. She faced losing her position and her life.

Yet, with encouragement from her Uncle Mordecai, she embraced the way of strength and courage. She declared, "*If I perish, I perish,*" and risked everything to save her people. Her bravery and faith turned the tide and led to a great victory.

Daniel had followed God all his life. Yet, when evil men sought his downfall, he chose to follow God rather than the ways of man. He faced death for refusing to obey the King's command to worship false gods.

Even when threatened with being thrown into the lions' den, Daniel did not waver. His trust in God saved him from the lions, and the King decreed that all must honour the God of Daniel.

While Daniel faced immediate danger, others faced different kinds of fear.

When God commanded Noah to build an ark in preparation for a great flood, there was no water in sight. Yet Noah followed God, and day after day, week after week, he built and crafted the ark, all while enduring the derision of those around him. He trusted God's plan, even when it must have been hard to understand God's purpose.

When Israelite spies came to the city of Jericho, Rahab, a prostitute, chose to hide them despite the grave danger if caught.

Because of her courage, Rahab and her family were spared when Jericho fell, and she became part of Jesus' lineage. Her story reminds us that God can redeem any past when we choose faith over fear.

Gideon was so fearful of his family and the men of his town that when God called him to destroy his father's altar of Baal, that he did it by night. Yet later, he would face an army of 135,000 with just 300 men.

It's worth noting that 32,000 men initially rallied to Gideon's call. But when God instructed Gideon to allow those who were 'fearful and trembling' to return home, only 10,000 men remained. God then further reduced the army to just 300 men.

Despite his fears and doubts, Gideon chose to keep trusting God and ultimately witnessed a miraculous victory.

Sometimes the greatest moments of faith come when we feel at our weakest or most human. Before Jesus went to the cross, arguably the greatest act of courage in human history, He too would wrestle with fear. He showed us the real courage is not the absence of fear, but choosing to trust God in the face of our fears.

Jesus was fully God, yet also fully human. In the garden of Gethsemane, facing His imminent crucifixion, He knew what it was to experience fear.

He prayed, *"Father, if you are willing, take this cup from me."* His anguish was so great that Luke's gospel tells us His sweat fell like drops of blood.

Yet, knowing the suffering that lay ahead of Him, Jesus chose to surrender to God's will, saying *"Yet not my will, but yours be done."*

Jesus faced His fear and went willingly to the cross. His example shows us that faith doesn't mean an absence of fear, but rather choosing God's will even in our most difficult moments.

These stories remind us that overcoming fear is possible. Not only is it possible, but it can be a gateway to great things for the Kingdom of God.

Just as so many of our Bible men and women did, we must choose courage and strength over anxiety and fear.

Unleashing our creativity requires us to trust God, putting ourselves in His hands, surrendering our own desires and allowing Him to lead and guide us.

Practical Steps to Overcome Fear

Overcoming fear isn't something we do just once, it's a process, something that we do minute after minute, hour after hour, day after day.

Fear kills hopes and dreams. As Les Brown said, *"Too many of us are not living our dreams, because we are living our fears."*

You can't do both - you can't live your dreams and your fears. We can learn to conquer fears in our lives, and overcome anxiety. The abundant life that He has called us to is not just some wild dream, it can be your reality.

But you need to act. Here are some practical steps you can take to deal with your fears:

Recognise Your Fear - become aware of the sensations of fear or anxiety, uncomfortable as they may feel initially. This can be the hardest thing.

We have become so used to feeling fearful or anxious, that we've never dared to face them and look directly at them.

Breathe! - as you become aware that you're feeling fearful or anxious, your heart rate may start to climb, your breathing may become more rapid, and you may feel tension gripping your body.

This is your body's stress response to fear and anxiety. You can learn to counter this by using some simple breathing techniques.

What is it that you're afraid of? If you find that question hard to answer, examine the thoughts that are filling your mind. Become aware of the fears that you are experiencing.

What is the worst thing that could happen? Allow your mind to go there, to that dark place, where the worst possible thing happens.

What is the best thing that could happen, once you conquer your fears? Picture this for a moment, in your mind.

Where do you believe God is leading you? What direction does He want you to take?

You may be able to answer this immediately, or you may need to patiently wait and ask Him for an answer. Once you become aware of where you feel God is leading you, you're ready for the next step.

Surrender to Him - give up your desires and your will.

You've thought about the worst thing that could happen, and imagined the best thing that might happen. Do you have a sense of where God is leading you?

CS Lewis put it like this, *"The terrible thing, the almost impossible thing, is to hand over your whole self - all your wishes and precautions - to Christ."*

Of all the steps, this may be the hardest.

When two paths lie in front of you, you have a choice. You can choose the one which appeals because it seems easier and safer or you can choose the one where you feel God may be leading.

Draw Your Line in the sand, once you've made your choice. There's no going back. Whatever your decision or choice, write it down, tell someone, make yourself accountable.

Stay Strong - over the next few hours, days or weeks, you will be tempted to doubt the choice or decision you have made today. You may wonder if it was just some crazy whim, whether you are taking the wrong path.

Jesus called us to follow him, wherever that may lead. If your heart's desire is to follow Christ, and your actions and decisions reflect this, is there really a wrong path?

Face the Battle - it's now that a battle begins, the battle in your mind. It's now that doubts and fears try to sneak back inside your mind.

The enemy will try to take you back over those oh so familiar thoughts and fears, to fight that battle all over again. So, there is one more question to ask yourself, which is this.

Guard Your Mind: Where is your focus? What thoughts are you allowing to fill your mind? When those fears arise, how will you handle them?

Here's a clue, just boot them out and tell them you've already made your choice, that your mind is made up.

This process may take minutes, days or weeks to work through, before you come to a place of faith.

Still Struggling?

If you find yourself still struggling to overcome your fears, remember that you are not alone. King David also cried out to God in his distress, and God answered him, freeing him from all his fears.

Psalm 34:4-5 gives us a powerful key to overcoming fear:

> *"I cried to God in my distress and he answered me. He freed me from all my fears! Gaze upon him, join your life with his, and joy will come. Your faces will glisten with glory. You'll never wear that shame-face again."*
>
> PSALM 34:4-5 (TPT)

So, cry out to God. Look at Him, join your life with His, and trust that joy will come.

Be patient with yourself, taking steps of faith and courage will get easier the more times you do it.

One day you'll look back to see that the worst thing you imagined never actually happened and see all the good things that happened, which you could never have anticipated.

From Fear to Joy in Creativity

As we learn to overcome our fears in creativity, we open ourselves up to a deep source of joy.

As creative Christ-followers, we will face unique challenges. But by relying on the Holy Spirit and taking steps of faith, we can step into the creative life God has for us.

You're not alone in your fears, and you don't have to stay stuck in them. If you will have the courage to face them, to call out to God, He promises to answer.

Put simply, choosing to follow a path of creativity is to choose joy.

As author Elizabeth Gilbert discovered in her own creative journey, *"A creative life is an amplified life. It's a bigger life, a happier life, an expanded life, and a … more interesting life."*

By choosing to face our fears and step into our creativity, we're choosing far more than just to make or create something – we're choosing to experience joy, as we experience the presence and guidance of the Holy Spirit.

People sometimes speak of this as the 'creative flow', which is another way we can experience joy.

The creative flow is so much more than any one moment – it's an invitation to participate in the ongoing act of creating, mirroring the Creator's own joy in bringing beauty, truth and goodness into the world.

The joy of being 100% focused on the act of creation is a simple joy that few things compare to.

Being creative also allows us to share our authentic selves with the world. If you feel that the world doesn't know or understand you, creativity may be a way of helping people get a glimpse of the real you.

There's much focus on mindfulness to help us find peace, but little said about how creativity can help us find peace and joy in our lives.

In a world obsessed with the past and the future, creativity gives you the joy and peace that comes with living in the moment fully. Not looking forward or back, but living fully in the moment.

As you step out, you'll start to experience more of the joy and peace that God promises you.

Each step of faith you take is not just a step away from fear, but a step towards the deep and lasting joy that comes from living out your creative calling.

In the end, creativity is not about perfection, but about connection – connection to your own true self, to those around you, and to the Father.

It's time to conquer your fear and embrace your creativity. Let's step out in faith together.

Over To You

Which Bible character do you most relate to and why?

....

....

....

What negative beliefs about your creativity have you been carrying? What would it look like to replace those with God's truth?

....
....
....

Take a moment to write down truths from God's Word that confirm your identity as His creative child.

....
....
....

ELEVEN
BUILD YOUR CREATIVE CONFIDENCE

So, you love the idea of being more creative, but something's holding you back?

Maybe it's fear of failure. Perhaps it's a fear of what others will think or say.

Maybe you think you're simply not good enough? Perhaps you long for approval, but creativity has only ever brought disapproval?

What are the deep-seated beliefs or experiences that are keeping you from fully embracing your creative potential?

Is it a harsh word spoken over you in childhood that you've remembered for all these years? Is it the voice in your head that whispers, *"Who do you think you are?"* when you dare to dream or imagine? Or perhaps it's the fear of stepping out of your comfort zone and trying something new, only to fall flat on your face.

Whatever it is that's holding you back, you're not alone. We all carry creative wounds, hurts and scars that can make us hesitate to step out in faith.

But here's the good news: your Heavenly Father came to heal those wounds and hurts. He came to give you the strength to overcome your fears and insecurities.

As He looks at you, He sees a beloved child, full of creative potential just waiting to be expressed.

And today, He's inviting you to let go of those doubts and fears, to step into the creative destiny He has for you.

Understanding Your Creative Blocks

The things that block our creativity often run deeper than we think, and go back farther than we realise.

What we believe about ourselves matters.

Renowned psychologist, Albert Bandura, came up with a theory to explain the saying we may be so familiar with, *"whether or not you believe you can, you're right."* His theory of self-efficacy says that your beliefs about yourself affect your performance.

You've probably seen this at work in others. Maybe you know someone who believes they can change the world, and they set out to do just that. Or someone who believes that they have little worth, lives out a life which reflects that belief.

Bandura's theory suggests that you'll only try things you believe you can be successful at. Yet, every artist or creator will experience failure.

Thomas Edison, inventor of the light bulb, famously said, *"I have not failed. I have just found 10,000 ways that won't work."*

He had created inventions that didn't work. Yet, rather than seeing his failed attempts as defeats, he saw them as steps toward eventual success.

Consider these examples: Oprah Winfrey was fired from her first television job as an anchor. Lucille Ball was dismissed from drama school for being too shy.

Vera Wang failed to make the US Olympic skating team and was passed over for a position with Vogue. J.K. Rowling's Harry Potter manuscripts were rejected by 12 publishers. Madonna was told she didn't have the talent to become a singer.

By the world's standards, each of these now-famous names failed. Yet, they didn't give up when faced with failure. They believed they had something to offer the world, so they persisted.

What you believe you can achieve is often shaped by those around you. If others expect you to fail, you're likely to believe them. But if they believe in your success, that confidence can become your own.

Your past performance, your experience of watching others, and your own expectations also shape your beliefs.

If you feel anxious and expect to fail, you probably will. On the other hand, if you are hopeful and believe you can succeed, you're more likely to achieve your goals.

Now that we understand how beliefs shape our creative potential, let's explore how to change those limiting beliefs.

Changing What You Believe About Yourself

You may have felt that your creativity was stifled somewhere along the way, or that a part of you got lost in the journey from childhood to adulthood. But here's the truth: your creativity is not lost, it's just waiting to be rediscovered and unleashed.

Perhaps you think it's too late for you to explore your creativity, that you've left it dormant for too long? Or maybe you're hesitating to explore your creativity because you feel like a beginner.

If so, you're not alone. Winston Churchill once said something profound about this common fear, "*Often, when we say it is 'too late' for us to begin something, what we are really saying is that we aren't willing to be a beginner.*

But when we are willing to dip our toe in, even just a little, we are rewarded with a sense of youthful wonder. Never give in, never give in, never, never, never, never."

Churchill's words are a powerful reminder that embracing the discomfort of being a beginner is often the key to unlocking our creative potential.

So how do you get past those beliefs that you're not creative or that your creative efforts have no worth or value?

While there's nothing you can do to change your past performance and experiences, you can change your perspective on the past.

Each failure has taught you things about yourself and about the world around you and the people in it.

You've learned something with each failure. You're not the same person you were before.

As Stephen Pressfield so eloquently puts it, every artist has to face their fears:

"Are you paralysed with fear? That's a good sign. Fear is good. Like self-doubt, fear is an indicator. Fear tells us what we have to do. Remember one rule of thumb: the more scared we are of a work or calling, the more sure we can be that we have to do it."

It can seem like an impossible challenge to overcome your fears to express your inner creativity, to create something of worth.

But it's possible to push past the fears, push past the resistance you feel, by putting in the effort, by persisting even when it's not always smooth going.

Remember, it may not always feel 'safe', but there's a joy that comes from expressing your inner creativity that's unlike anything else. Embracing that joy is worth facing up to your fears.

Renewing Your Mind with God's Truth

You can choose to surround yourself with people who believe in you, who cheer you on. But most importantly, your Heavenly Father believes in you, even when all you feel are doubts or fears. If you have Him alone, He is more than enough.

The Bible encourages us to renew our mind, because it knows that the Word has power to transform our thinking. You can allow your heavenly Father's belief in you to change and transform your belief in yourself.

This isn't some new age mumbo-jumbo. It's simply believing that what He's put inside you, through the power of His Holy Spirit, is greater than your own fears and anxieties. It's believing that His power in you is greater than you can imagine.

It's looking to Him and understanding how great and awesome He is. He has put the seeds of creativity inside you that have the power to transform your thinking.

Immerse yourself in the truth of what your Heavenly Father says about you. Embrace these truths and accept that you are loved. Counter the arguments of the enemy with Bible truths. Remember, His strength is greater than your weakness.

How about taking Bandura's theory and making it your own? Instead of saying "*whether or not I believe I can, I'm right,*" change it to "*whether or not I believe He can, I'm right.*"

Will you choose to believe His word about you? Choose to believe in all that He speaks over you? Will you set aside your own fears and doubts and trust the Holy Spirit power inside you?

It's a choice you can make, one that you'll need to make every single day.

Your Hidden Potential

Have you ever considered the humble acorn? It's so small that you can easily hold it in the palm of your hand.

Yet, locked up inside each tiny acorn is all the potential to become a mighty oak tree. A tree which, given the right circumstances, could one day tower above you, reaching high into the sky.

Each acorn is a tiny miracle, yet when was the last time you stopped and looked in awe at an acorn or the mighty oak it could become? We so easily take nature's miracles for granted.

The same is true for you. You are one of God's amazing miracles, with incredible potential locked up inside you.

You have within you everything you need to become the person God wants you to be and accomplish the things He's placed on your heart - and this potential is powered by something greater than yourself.

Inside you is the creative power that brought the universe into being. Inside you is the creative power that formed you in your mother's womb. Inside you is the creative power that by a single touch brings life, joy and peace.

If you allow the Holy Spirit's power to flow in your life, you don't have to try harder. If you'll learn to listen to His voice and follow where He leads, you will discover unexpected strength. If you remove any rocks from the stream, the Holy Spirit can flow freely.

You already have everything you need.

Your Creative Journey

Now that you're beginning to understand what's been holding you back and how to move forward, close your eyes for a moment. Picture yourself setting out on an adventure, you don't know what you'll discover, but you know that the journey to discovery will be fun.

Your Heavenly Father has put unique skills, passions and desires within you. No-one is quite the same as you. You're unique. You're special.

Don't you owe it to yourself, and to the world, to discover this unique and special person God has created you to be? Instead of hiding your light under a bushel, is it time to embrace that light and allow it to shine?

Are you ready to step out on the path of creativity and discover the gifts God has placed inside you?

Over To You

How are your self-beliefs limiting your creative potential?

………………………………………………………………………

………………………………………………………………………

………………………………………………………………………

What small creative act could you try this week?

………………………………………………………………………

………………………………………………………………………

………………………………………………………………………

TWELVE
REMOVING THE BOULDERS

As a child, I can remember the joy of placing stones and rocks in a stream, to block the flow. My sister and I loved nothing more than to wander about barefoot, damming the river's flow.

The greatest joy came when our parents said it was time to go and we got to release the water which had built up - often by removing just one or two larger stones.

God used this picture to speak to me about the flow of the Holy Spirit in my own life. It made me realise that we can block the flow of His Holy Spirit, just as easily as my sister and I could block the flow of the stream.

Have you ever felt like the flow of God's Spirit in your life has diminished to a trickle? Does it sometimes feel as if there are obstacles blocking the once free-flowing stream of His presence and power? If you have, you're not alone.

Unblocking The Flow

As creative beings made in God's image, we're meant to experience the free flow of His Spirit in our lives. Yet sometimes, that flow can become blocked.

As we journey through life, it's easy to accumulate what I call "*boulders*" that hinder the Holy Spirit's work in and through us.

In this chapter, we'll explore what these boulders might look like and how they can limit our ability to live out our God-given creativity.

We'll use the analogy of a stream to understand how even small obstructions can eventually dam up the flow.

But there's good news: God wants to help us identify and remove these boulders, so that we can once again experience the fullness of His Spirit. Get ready to do some boulder-blasting and unleash a rushing river of God's power in your life!

Just like physical rocks and stones can obstruct the flow of a stream, there are things in our spiritual lives that can block the flow of the Holy Spirit.

These "*boulders*" might be unconfessed sins, unforgiveness, believing lies about ourselves, or failing to fully surrender our lives to God.

Our Christian journey can start out much like a babbling brook, flowing freely and unencumbered with clean fresh water.

As we go through life, we or others can place boulders that block the flow of the stream. After a while, there are so many rocks and boulders, that the stream's flow is reduced to a trickle.

At first, these issues might seem small, like pebbles that barely affect the stream. But over time, as more and more accumulate, the flow starts to get hindered.

Eventually, what was once a strongly flowing river can become a stagnant trickle. The boulders have built up, and the life-giving flow is blocked.

As you become more reliant on the Holy Spirit to lead and guide you in your creativity, you may become aware that the flow of the Holy Spirit is not what you would desire it to be. Perhaps you sense that it's not what it used to be.

We can blame it on life's busyness, but the reality is that we've failed to tend the stream, to remove the rocks and boulders that have accumulated. We've allowed ourselves to be satisfied with the trickle of God's spirit, instead of longing for more.

The Impact on Our Creativity

The gifting and calling of God don't change (Romans 11:29). But we can limit the expression of our gifting by our actions or failure to deal with these rocks and boulders.

There's no blame or shame. We all accumulate boulders in our lives, even though we may not be aware of them. Even when we are, we may feel powerless to remove them. We may go months or even years, living with them, accepting them as the norm.

It's then that we need to 'do business' with our Heavenly Father - to come to Him and ask Him to show us the way forward. Jesus shared a prayer that can help keep our life free from hindrances.

The Lord's Prayer shows us some of the things which can become 'boulders' in our life.

The prayer starts with these familiar words:

> *Our Father in heaven* – a reminder of who our heavenly Father is and, just as importantly, who you are
>
> *Your will be done* - which speaks about living life His way, rather than our own
>
> *Give us this day our daily bread* - a reminder to give our worries and cares to Him and to trust Him for all that we need today
>
> *Forgive us our debts* - this is an opportunity for a daily cleaning of the slate. To bring to him our failings and shortcomings. To confess to Him those times when we've messed up or the times when we've gone in the opposite direction from where He was leading us.
>
> *As we also have forgiven our debtors* - this speaks about unforgiveness in our hearts. It tells us that, when we harbour unforgiveness in our hearts, we cannot expect to live in the fullness of life empowered by Him.

Unforgiveness is probably the most insidious boulder of all and the most challenging to deal with.

Lead us not into temptation, but deliver us from evil - we all succumb to temptations of lose our way on the path, have to re-focus and find our way once more.

In one prayer, our Heavenly Father identifies issues that can block our spiritual flow. These include our identity in Him, trusting Him with our worries and cares, asking for forgiveness when we make mistakes or succumb to temptation, and the necessity of forgiving others as we ourselves have been forgiven.

Perhaps you're aware of other things which block the flow of the Holy Spirit in your life?

Unblocking Your Stream

Before we look at how God removes these boulders, take a moment to reflect on these questions:

What boulders are blocking your stream?

Are there worries and cares that you are carrying, that you need to give to Him?

Are you believing lies that you or others have spoken to or over you? If so, can you identify the turning point where the lies got in to your mind and heart?

Is there shame that you need to ask Him to heal in your life?

Are you aware of unforgiveness or anger in your heart, that you need to deal with?

Are you conscious of any unconfessed sins, that you need to bring to the Father?

Will you ask Him to show you what's blocking the flow of His Holy Spirit in your life?

You may not even realise what the boulders or blockages are, until He sheds His light on them.

There's no one-size fits all solution. He will deal with each rock or boulder in your life in the way that's just right for you, at the time that's right for you.

God is the only One who can show us the way and empower us remove these 'boulders' which block the flow of his Holy Spirit in our lives.

If you ask Him, He will reveal the boulders in your life and show you a way to remove them. He might reveal it when you're in a time of worship in church or as you're driving the car. He might reveal it as you're pottering around the house. He might reveal it through the well-meaning words of a friend.

He may reveal it as you read the words of the Bible. He may reveal it when you least expect it. However revelation comes, it will come. He is faithful and will show you at just the right time.

Once you realise there is a boulder obstructing the flow of the Holy Spirit in your life, you have a choice.

You can respond and allow him, by his power to remove it. Or you can try to ignore it, resist and allow the boulder to remain. Whatever you choose, God will not force anything on you.

The moment He reveals each boulder, I believe He also gives the power to overcome and remove that boulder. In that moment of revelation, also comes His power.

As he brings things to light, will you whisper a quiet yes of surrender to him? Will you open up your heart and allow him to do any heart surgery that's needed? He will be faithful to do it, if you will only say yes to Him.

Do you trust that He is able to do what you have been unable to do for weeks, months or years? When you sense Him revealing a boulder in your life, it comes back to a question of trust.

Are you willing to confess that you've been walking the wrong path, and ask Him the strength to turn around and choose a different path?

Will you release to him your worries and cares allow him to carry them for you?

Will you accept and embrace your identity as His beloved child?

He wants to lead and guide you at every step of the journey. He longs to be present in your life. He desires to fill you with his Holy Spirit power.

As you stand at this moment of choice, remember that unblocking the flow of the Holy Spirit in your life isn't about perfection—it's about surrender.

Your Heavenly Father wants to clear away those boulders and set you free.

Each small 'yes' you whisper opens the way for His healing power to flow, bringing you closer to the abundant life He's prepared just for you.

Over To You

Invite the Holy Spirit to reveal anything that might be blocking your creative flow. What boulder is the Holy Spirit revealing to you right now? What would it look like to trust Him to remove it?

……………………………………………………………………
……………………………………………………………………
……………………………………………………………………

Did any of the following resonate with you - trust, forgiveness, shame, believing lies, or unconfessed sin? If so, are you ready to say 'yes' to allowing Him to help you remove these boulders?

……………………………………………………………………
……………………………………………………………………
……………………………………………………………………

THIRTEEN
LIVING A LIFE OF CREATIVITY

When you start the process of removing any boulders, you open yourself up to the possibility of a greater joy and freedom in your walk with God. You may discover a new sense of passion and purpose.

As you open your heart to the flow of His Spirit, you are poised to receive His creative promptings and direction.

With this newfound freedom, you are ready to embark on your creative journey and explore and express the unique gifts He has placed within you.

Finding Time for Creativity

One challenge for many of us is finding time for creativity in our busy lives. In today's fast-paced world, it often feels like there's never enough time to pursue our creative passions.

Creativity takes time. Yet, time is the one thing that we all seem to be short of. We're constantly juggling all the demands on our time - work, family and other responsibilities, which leaves little room for exploring our creativity.

It's as if creativity has been replaced by busyness. We're so busy that it's not always easy to find time to be creative.

We tell ourselves that we'll do it later, or that we'll do it when the kids grow up, or when we retire. But the truth is, 'later' never seems to come.

As Maya Angelou said, *"You can't use up creativity. The more you use, the more you have."*

When I wanted to write my book, Women of Courage, (which explores the stories of 31 women from the Bible) I honestly didn't see how I had the time to do so.

So, I took a long, slow look at my schedule. I realised that every Wednesday afternoon I took my dog for a long walk.

I found time on a Monday and Tuesday evening to read and make notes in preparation.

Each Wednesday when I walked my dog Bruno, I'd pray, asking the Holy Spirit for insight into each woman's story.

When I arrived home, I'd sit at the computer and write it all down.

It may seem strange that I had to 'plan in' creativity, but I believe that this is the reality of modern life.

If we don't intentionally make space for creativity, it's all too easy for it to get pushed aside by the demands of the day.

If it's not scheduled, it's probably not going to happen.

There's No Map

As you begin to explore and express your God-given creativity, you'll start to experience a deep inner joy and satisfaction.

Franklin D. Roosevelt put this feeling into words, when he said, *"Happiness lies in the joy of achievements and the thrill of creative effort."*

There's no map for your journey, but there is a guide. As you lean in and listen for His voice, He will faithfully guide and direct you. Whether it's through a `bible verse or an inner conviction, He'll show you the next step or reveal the end goal.

Every journey looks different. Your journey will be different to mine. Ruth's journey was very different from Rahab's journey, and Esther's journey was different from Martha's journey, yet each one was faithful to the call of God on their lives.

Only you can find your way. Only you can discover your next step and explore the things your Heavenly Father has in store for you.

So, embrace your unique path and trust Him to guide you each step of the way.

One Day At A Time

In the Lord's Prayer, which we know so well, it says, "*give us this day our daily bread*". Notice that it doesn't say this week's bread, it says our 'daily bread'.

Our Heavenly Father doesn't promise to give us what we need for tomorrow, or next week. He promises to give you all that you need for 'this day', that means *today*.

He promises to give you the courage, the wisdom and the strength to do all that He's put in your heart *today*.

So, as you continue your creative journey, remember to:

- *Walk closely* with Him, being thankful that you can call yourself His child
- *Believe* that you are who He says you are
- *Ask* the Holy Spirit to work through you
- *Celebrate* your unique gifts and stop comparing yourself with others
- *Be courageous*, kick fear aside, and breathe deeply

Then simply begin!

Your Next Step

You're probably familiar with the saying "*a journey of 1000 miles begins with a single step*".

Yet, getting started is often the most challenging part of any journey. Taking that first step can feel completely overwhelming.

Our fears quickly rise up like monsters, making everything in us want to run in the opposite direction - much like Jonah trying to escape his calling.

I get it. These fears can be paralysing, making it difficult to take action.

We become masters of procrastination, putting things off until another day, because we can't see every step in the journey. It's all too easy to feel intimidated by the size of the task ahead of us. To fear failure.

The unknown can feel daunting. We can fear getting lost along the way. We can fear facing seemingly impossible obstacles or encountering setbacks.

Deep down, a nagging voice whispers that we're not good enough, not capable enough.

But here's the truth. It's at times like this, facing our own fears and uncertainties that we get the opportunity to exercise the muscles of faith. These moments of doubt and hesitation are actually sacred opportunities to grow and deepen our trust in God.

But God doesn't call those who are already equipped, He equips those that He calls. When we listen to His voice, He promises to provide everything we need.

As we delight in Him, He promises to give us the desires of our heart (Psalm 37:4). When we delight in something, we find joy and pleasure in it. As we find our joy in Him, that joy will overflow into our creativity.

So, when you sense fear rising up, remember, this is your opportunity to trust God. It's your opportunity to grow in your faith, to lean in and listen for His voice and to follow where He leads.

Trust that the same God who gave Bezalel the skills to craft His temple, and who raised Jesus from the dead, is more than able to give you all you need to bring your dreams to life.

So, take that first small step. You don't need to see the entire path, simply trust that God will guide you, one step at a time.

Believe His "I Will Make You"

Jesus asked His followers, "*Who do you say that I am?*" (Matthew 16:15 NIV)

It's time for you to ask your heavenly Father that same question, who do you say that I am? It may be days since you started following Jesus, or it may be years. What will following Him mean for you?

What single step can you take today towards fulfilling the calling and gifting He's placed inside you? One day you'll stand before the throne of God and give an account of yourself (Romans 14:12).

Although no-one but Jesus measures up to God's standard, we can all do something with the little we've been given.

When we're faithful with what He's placed in our hands, whether little or much, we are more likely to hear those beautiful words, "*Well done, good and faithful servant … Enter into the joy of your master* (Matthew 25:23)."

And that faithfulness often starts with a simple question – the same one God asked Moses when he felt inadequate for the task ahead: What's in your hand?

When Moses felt fearful about relaying what God had said to Pharaoh, God asked him, *"What is that in your hand?"* (Exodus 4:2). God commanded Moses to throw the staff in his hand to the ground where it turned into a serpent.

God used this as a sign to Moses and to everyone else, that God had appeared to him. It was also to be a sign to Pharaoh, who was holding the Israelites in captivity.

Just as God used Moses's simple shepherd's staff, Jesus took ordinary fishermen and turned their lives around. When Jesus called the disciples, He asked them what they had in their hand. He promised them, "*I will make you fishers of men*" (Matthew 4:19).

Notice that Jesus didn't say "*become fishers of men*" - He said "*I will make you*." The transformation would come not through their own efforts, but through simply walking with Jesus.

In Jesus' day, rabbis taught their disciples by spending time with them. The disciples would see how their rabbi lived, listen to his teaching, and learn to follow his ways. But unlike other rabbis who said "*learn from me*," Jesus said "*follow me*." He invited them into a relationship, not just a classroom.

Jesus often led His disciples into places or situations that would make them feel uncomfortable - touching those with leprosy, speaking with the Samaritan woman, and eating with tax collectors.

Yet, their greatest growth happened precisely in those moments of discomfort. Just as the disciples learned to trust Jesus beyond their comfort zones, He invites us to do the same with our creativity - to step out in faith, even when it feels uncomfortable or unfamiliar.

These simple fishermen would experience both triumphs and failures in their journey with Jesus.

At times, they were amazed by God's power working through them, exclaiming "*Lord, even the demons are subject to us in your name!*" (Luke 10:17).

Yet at other times, they faced disappointment, asking "*Why couldn't we drive it out?*" (Matthew 17:19) when they failed to heal a demon-possessed boy.

Jesus's disciples denied Him, deserted Him, and argued with each other about who would be the greatest. They were far from perfect, yet they were the ones that Jesus chose.

That should give us hope. We don't have to be perfect for us to be used by God.

Just as the disciples were transformed by spending time with Jesus, it's the same for us. As we spend time with Him, we will be changed by Him. We don't have to strive or struggle to transform ourselves - we simply need to follow where He leads.

Your part is simply to follow Him, to spend time with Him. His part is to shape you into who He's called you to be - that's why He promises "*I will make you*".

Over To You

What creative activity brings you the most joy?

....
....
....

What's one way you can create space for creativity in your daily or weekly routine?

....
....
....

How might your life look different if you truly believed Jesus is actively transforming you, rather than trying to transform yourself?

....
....
....

FOURTEEN
YOUR JOURNEY BEGINS

As you begin to explore your God-given creativity, you may be surprised where He might lead you!

As you trust God with your gifts and allow His Spirit to lead you, I believe you'll discover greater joy, peace and purpose in your life.

As you begin to live out your creative calling, watch and see the ripple effect, as you start to inspire and encourage those around you.

Your Heavenly Father is inviting you to join Him in the work of creating, to partner with Him in bringing more of His light and beauty into the world. Will you say yes?

Following Him is a path which can lead to a life of greater freedom, joy and contentment. Only by following where He leads, can you know the sense of fulfilment your heart yearns for.

He encourages you to let tomorrow take care of itself and focus only on what you can do today.

What step can you take on your creative journey today?

So take that first step, and then the next.

Keep following the Creator's lead, one faithful step at a time.

As you step out in faith and embrace the unique creativity God has placed within you, get ready to be amazed at what He will do.

BECOMING A CHRIST FOLLOWER

Throughout this book, we've explored how creativity is deeply woven into our identity as children of God.

We've discovered that creativity isn't about more than creating, but about bringing hope and reflecting God's creative nature.

Just as creativity requires courage to step into the unknown, following Jesus is a similar journey of faith. It's about believing that something beautiful can emerge from what might feel broken or damaged.

God doesn't just want to be the inspiration for your creativity; He wants you to join His family.

He wants to restore and renew your life. God loves and accepts you, as you are, and wants to have a relationship with you.

Would you like to become part of the family of God? Would you like to know for sure who you really are?

Are you ready to put the past behind you and trust God for your future?

The Bible tells us that *"God so loved the world, that he gave his only Son, that whoever believes in him should not perish but have eternal life.*

For God did not send his Son into the world to condemn the world, but in order that the world might be saved through him."(John 3:16–17, NIV)

God, the Father, sent His Son, Jesus, to rescue you — to bring you into His family. You are loved by God and precious to Him.

Are you ready to make a choice to follow Jesus Christ?

If you feel ready, you can make the choice to follow Jesus Christ right now.

You can know God's love and forgiveness. Because of what Jesus did, you can be accepted into God's family by praying this simple prayer:

Father,

I am sorry for the things I have done wrong.

Thank you that Jesus died for me, rose from the dead, and is alive today.

Please forgive me for living life my own way.

Please come into my life and fill me with your Holy Spirit.

I accept Jesus Christ as my Lord and Saviour.

I choose to follow Him today and every day.

Amen

If you have prayed this prayer from your heart, you are forgiven. All the wrong things you have ever done have been taken away. You're a child of God, loved and accepted by your Heavenly Father.

This is the start of a new life, a life strengthened by the power of the Holy Spirit.

You have a new identity as a child of God, you're part of His family now. Every promise from God the Father applies to you.

What Do I Do Now?

Tell someone! If you know other Christ-followers, tell one of them that you have prayed this prayer.

Find and read your Bible. If you don't have one, get a hold of one or download a Bible app on your phone.

Get involved in a local church. A good church will help you to grow and learn as a Christ-follower.

Seek out wise Christians and don't be afraid to ask questions. Consider joining an Alpha course, which is a safe place to ask your questions.

Pray. Talk to God, thank Him for the good things, ask Him to guide you, forgive others, and ask Him for your daily needs.

Making the decision to follow Jesus is the most important choice you will ever make. It's a choice that will not only transform your life here on earth but will also ensure your eternal future with Him.

As you grow in your relationship with Him, you will begin to discover the abundant life He has in store for you – a life filled with purpose and hope.

As you step out in faith and trust the Creator to work in and through you, remember that He is faithful and His love for you is unfailing.

He can and will give you everything you need to become the unique person He created you to be.

Your creative journey doesn't end here - it's just beginning. And this time, you're no longer alone, but walking with the Creator Himself.

ABOUT THE AUTHOR

My own journey to creativity has completely transformed my life and brought so much unexpected joy!

I believe that you are uniquely designed by God with a creative purpose, and that unleashing this creativity can be a powerful way to reflect His nature and make an impact on the world.

I believe that as you step out in faith and allow your creativity to flourish, you will experience a new level of joy, purpose, and intimacy with your Creator.

My hope is that this book has inspired you to discover and pursue the creative dreams God has placed in your heart, trusting Him to guide and equip you every step of the way.

On a personal note, I have three grown-up children and ten grandchildren. I enjoy spending time at my beachside apartment in the south of England and at my country cottage in Sweden.

When I'm not writing, you can often find me exploring nature, trying out a new creative hobby, or enjoying deep conversations with friends and family.

You may enjoy some of my other books, including:

Women of Courage - find inspiration and courage through thirty-one biblical women who faced their own impossible situations. Their stories will encourage you to walk boldly with God, whatever you're facing.

Daily Readings for Difficult Days - short daily readings to bring peace and hope when life feels overwhelming. Whether you're facing divorce, loss or depression, find daily comfort and encouragement to keep going and hold onto faith.

Meeting Jesus - journey alongside nine remarkable women from the Bible whose lives were changed by their encounters with Jesus. Discover how Jesus' touch can bring hope, healing, and purpose to your own life, just as it did for these women centuries ago.

Learning to Live in Challenging Times - through the timeless biblical story of Ruth and Naomi, discover encouragement for navigating life's challenges, assurance that their story matters, and guidance for finding hope and purpose even in unexpected circumstances.

Watch and Listen - you may also enjoy some of my YouTube videos. These include spoken word, thoughts on Christian life and vlogs from my cottage in Sweden.

facebook.com/jennifercarterwriter
bookbub.com/authors/jennifer-carter
youtube.com/JenniferCarterWriter

ONE MORE THING

Thanks for taking time to read or listen to this book. If you've enjoyed it, please consider leaving a rating or review.

I appreciate the time you've taken to read this book. As an independent author, it means a lot!

If you have 60 seconds, hearing your honest feedback on Amazon would mean the world to me. It does wonders for the book, and I love hearing about your experience with it.

www.ingramcontent.com/pod-product-compliance
Lightning Source LLC
Chambersburg PA
CBHW072100110526
44590CB00018B/3247